JOSSEY-BASS GUIDES
TO ONLINE TEACHING AND LEARNING

Conquering the Content

A Step-by-Step Guide to Online Course Design

Robin M. Smith

JOSSEY-BASS
A Wiley Imprint
www.josseybass.com

Published by Jossey-Bass
A Wiley Imprint
989 Market Street, San Francisco, CA 94103-1741—www.josseybass.com

Readers should be aware that Internet Web sites offered as citations and/or sources for further information may have changed or disappeared between the time this was written and when it is read.

Limit of Liability/Disclaimer of Warranty: While the publisher and author have used their best efforts in preparing this book, they make no representations or warranties with respect to the accuracy or completeness of the contents of this book and specifically disclaim any implied warranties of merchantability or fitness for a particular purpose. No warranty may be created or extended by sales representatives or written sales materials. The advice and strategies contained herein may not be suitable for your situation. You should consult with a professional where appropriate. Neither the publisher nor author shall be liable for any loss of profit or any other commercial damages, including but not limited to special, incidental, consequential, or other damages.

Jossey-Bass books and products are available through most bookstores. To contact Jossey-Bass directly call our Customer Care Department within the U.S. at 800-956-7739, outside the U.S. at 317-572-3986, or fax 317-572-4002.

Jossey-Bass also publishes its books in a variety of electronic formats. Some content that appears in print may not be available in electronic books.

Library of Congress Cataloging-in-Publication Data

Smith, Robin M., 1962-
    Conquering the content : a step-by-step guide to online course design / Robin M. Smith. — 1st ed.
        p. cm.
    Includes bibliographical references and index.
    ISBN 978-0-7879-9442-6 (pbk.)
    1. Web-based instruction—Design. 2. College teaching. I. Title.
    LB1044.87S617 2008
    378.1'7344678   2007050956

Printed in the United States of America
FIRST EDITION
PB Printing   10 9 8 7 6 5 4 3

Contents

7 Design with Navigation in Mind

Soli Deo Gloria!

Preface

Steven and his wife, Jenny, have three children: Drew, age five; Seth, age three; and Jessica, eighteen months. Steven, a police officer for the local police department, doesn't earn enough at his job to make ends meet. The city has tried to increase police salaries, but voters have rejected the last three tax initiatives. So Steven took on an additional job just over two years ago when they found out their third child was on the way.

Steven and Jenny decided they both need an education to improve their financial situation. Jenny is now in school full time; it costs more for her to put the children in day care than she has been able to find a job making, so she doesn't work. Steven took a third job, this one part time, to help pay for their tuition. Steven will get a raise when he completes his associate degree, which will allow them to afford the gas for him to commute to the university, which is forty miles away, one night a week. At the university he can eventually earn a four-year degree, which will lead to a better, higher-paying job that will support his family and allow them more stability. There is one problem: the only class he needs in order to graduate is biology with a lab; it meets five hours per week, and there is no way he can juggle all of his work schedules to be off that many hours each week. So far an entire semester and a summer have elapsed with no solution to this scheduling issue.

As providence would have it, the following fall, my biology course was offered online for the first time. Steven was in my course and faithfully logged in every night after work at 11:00 P.M. What an amazing opportunity this was for me to understand how important Web-based learning can be in the lives of students.

I've had the good fortune to be connected with countless students for whom Web-based learning has had a life-changing impact. These students have had an opportunity to get a degree from home rather than commute, which has allowed them to get an education that otherwise would have been impossible because of family responsibilities. I live in a rural state, where many individuals need to care for children or aging parents, or both, and may not have transportation reliable enough for a long commute. Web-based learning is making an economic impact on people and allowing them to make a better life for themselves and their children. It is amazing the complications against which students are struggling in order to obtain an education—particularly in first-generation college students.

For this reason, I want to reduce the burden of developing a Web-based course to the lowest possible level for faculty. If it is efficient and straightforward, more faculty can have an impact on students who need an opportunity to further their education without the constraints a normal classroom course imposes.

Originally I spent many hours trying to figure out how to get a course online and did many, many things wrong in the process. When I attempted to update my course the second semester, I realized how much I'd done wrong and spent countless hours correcting those mistakes. I determined then that I would do all I could to prevent faculty members within my scope of influence from going through the turmoil and frustrations I had just experienced. There was no reason for anyone else to have to figure out the things I had just learned the hard way. I began to show other faculty members on my own campus how to be organized from the beginning and how to create course content that was easily updatable and to use a system that would serve them for many semesters to come. Then I began expanding the training to show faculty members on other campuses how to do this work.

Many of us entered teaching in order to make a difference in the lives of people. I have seen the enormous difference Web-based courses can make to the students who are taking the courses and their families. I also understand the time constraints faculty have to deal with and the time investment required to develop a Web-based course. With faculty under pressure for so many responsibilities other than teaching, I knew an efficient and easy-to-follow development system was of the utmost importance to them in order for Web-based courses to be developed well and in a timely manner. *Conquering the Content* presents a collection of the tools and techniques I have used over the past decade in faculty development workshops.

When This Book Is Most Useful

In a perfect world, you would have this book nine to twelve months before your Web-based course is first offered online. You could begin in Chapter One and complete content presentations for each learning style and multimedia learning activities for each learning concept in your course until you've developed in perfect detail each of the modules of your course. However, reality tends to rear its ugly head and dictates that the great majority of faculty must select some portions of a course on which to focus and leave other portions for future development.

Fortunately, I've planned for those of us who live in an imperfect world. This entire development system revolves around selecting and developing the highest-priority items first, while leaving room for and adding other elements later as time allows (if it ever does). If time never allows, then you have the essential elements of the course online, and all is well. In addition, development of your course over time will give you the advantage of gaining experience at teaching online. This invaluable experience will have a beneficial effect on the way you update and continue to develop your Web-based course. Perhaps there are more benefits to our reality than we might have realized.

How This Book Is Organized

Each chapter begins by modeling use of the learning guides (an overview of learning outcomes and activities) by using these as your introduction to expected outcomes for each chapter.

Chapter One addresses how the learning environment is altered for Web-based learners versus classroom learners and the needs those differences create for content design. In addition, it asks you to identify the learning outcomes of the course you will be working on as you progress through this book.

In Chapter Two you will find out that everyone who develops a Web-based course is just as uncomfortable as you are at the beginning, so you don't have to be confident about this entire process to get through it. All you need is persistence and content expertise. The chapter also sets out the necessary information structures to make sure your course is developed for longevity and provides all you need now and in the future when you update the course. I want your course to be easily updatable and organized in such a way that you can add new components to the course as your skills and ideas grow.

Chapter Three addresses assessment issues and challenges you to move to higher levels beyond the typical objective tests. You will learn to develop assessments prior to designing the learning experiences. When you determine how students can demonstrate their knowledge, then you can create the appropriate learning experiences.

This system will assist you in designing your course from the student's point of view. A design that makes sure students know what to do at every point is the one that will lead to the most student success. Chapter Four therefore focuses on organization and learning guides. Creating well-developed learning guides is the key to a well-organized course for both you and your students.

The learning principles in Chapter Five are fundamental brain research principles that we've ignored too long in the education world. Chunking course content was a method I first used in 1996 in the classroom when I realized my students did not know how to study. I understood that if I could not help them learn how to study, I could not help them learn any of the subject matter we had before us. I have had more positive feedback from students in courses in which I've used these methods than any other way of teaching I've used.

Chapter Six shares some suggestions from my years of experience teaching online and cautions about some common pitfalls to avoid. Peer review of Web-based courses is also addressed in this chapter.

Chapter Seven focuses on navigation issues. Since *Conquering the Content* advocates the complete development of the course before placing materials online, navigation issues do not come into play until late in the process of development. Accomplishments and next steps are also outlined in this chapter. By this point, you will have completed the fundamentals of your entire course and be ready for a variety of future steps depending on your accomplishments to date.

Appendix A provides the forms you will progress through in order to develop your online course. These forms facilitate time on task, keep you on track, and help you to create a well-organized and pedagogically sound Web-based course as you progress thought this book.

Each chapter ends with action steps and a time estimate for accomplishing each step. Appendix B lists these steps in one place so you can get an overview of the amount of work to be done.

Appendix C provides a copy of the American Association for Higher Education's Principles of Good Practice for Assessing Student Learning. These will help you build better assessment or evaluation tasks for your students.

Appendix D presents a list of design and development tasks that need to be completed before each semester begins. Accomplishing these tasks will free you to concentrate on learning principles and student interactions during the semester.

The pages in the Notes section (Ideas for Application) after the appendices are to record your teaching ideas when they come to you while you are reading this book. Recording your ideas as they arise will help free your mind for further creativity rather than expending that cognitive load on remembering a list of ideas.

Whom This Book Can Benefit

This book will be useful for a range of people:

- Faculty members who need to develop a Web-based course and may be left on their own to accomplish this
- Faculty who want to supplement their classroom course with Web-based materials and need a sound organizational system for doing so
- Faculty who teach in the classroom and could benefit from:

  An organized way to file and retrieve course materials

  A process for making expectations clearer to students

  Content presentations that are conducive to learning
- Faculty with a preexisting Web-based course who need a design system for Web-based course development that is easy to update for new textbooks, new content, and new course materials
- Support units needing resources and tools to which to refer faculty in order to juggle their multiple duties
- Those who assist with course development but need additional references on organization and development aids
- Administrators who are trying to develop procedures and understand what is involved in developing a Web-based course
- Students in educational technology or distance learning programs
- Students in higher education degree programs

- Subject matter experts who will be teaching or desire to develop skills for transferring information to others
- Faculty and health care professionals who will be teaching or mentoring future professionals but have few opportunities for educational professional development

What This Book Does Not Do

Just as important as setting out what this book does is what it does not do:

- It does not address the technical aspects of any specific learning management system. Rather, it helps faculty prepare content that will work with any such system.
- It does not teach how to do what I call "mouse clicks" within any specific learning management system. Mouse clicks refer to the exact steps to accomplish particular tasks within the software. For example, I do not provide the steps to create quizzes or discussion topics within Blackboard, Desire2Learn, Angel, Moodle, and others.
- It does not address interacting with classmates, which is covered in other books (Palloff and Pratt, 1999, 2001, 2005; Conrad and Donaldson, 2004).
- It does not include the considerable administrative and support procedures and structures needed to manage a Web-based learning organization.
- It does not address design issues as they apply to color, graphics, and pleasing design of the content. I will mention some aspects of design that are significant because of learning issues, but I will not go through the aesthetics of what you are developing. My goal is that your course materials are online by the time you finish this book, and spending lots of time making them look artistic is a bonus for which you may not have time.

My Goal for This Book

As I developed my own Web-based courses, I noticed a large gap in the literature and in the practical application of information for exactly what to do with content in Web-based courses. No one was addressing the gorilla in the room. So that is my mission here: to give suggestions about what to do with that gorilla of content. I do not propose to have all the answers. I have a few answers that I hope will stimulate other ideas.

The ideas and methods contained in this book have been applied in courses scattered across the United States in the past decade, and they have met with success for faculty of many different disciplines. You will notice that some chapters of this book are noticeably shorter than others. That a chapter is brief signals that it either has less to do with presentation of content or I have less experience to share in those areas (or both). In areas where I have less hands-on experience, I suggest some reference materials for you to investigate. I can speak with authority and confidence on ideas I have tried and succeeded with or ideas I have tried and failed and retried and reworked until they were successful in practice. We can all read the research, but until it is put to the test of our own personal experience, it may or may not work with our teaching style and our own communities of practice. What works beautifully for the faculty member in the next office may fail miserably for me.

I would appreciate your feedback on your experience with *Conquering the Content*—both positive and negative, as well as suggestions for improvement. We are all learning even as we teach and add to our ideas each semester. It was difficult for me to find a stopping place and submit the manuscript to Jossey-Bass, my publisher, because I was constantly thinking of one more way to improve, and I did not want to end the conversation. Then I realized I could begin the conversation only after I presented these methods to a wider audience, so we can communicate with each other. I invite your comments at smithrobinm@uams.edu. Also, please join the Conquering the Content conversation by emailing me at smithrobinm@uams.edu.

The Author

Robin M. Smith is an instructional design specialist at the University of Arkansas for Medical Sciences in Little, Rock Arkansas, where she provides faculty and curriculum development for Web-based learning and teaching for faculty in the Colleges of Medicine, Pharmacy, Public Health, Nursing, and Health Related Professions as well as the Graduate School. She holds a Ph.D. in systematic entomology from Texas A&M University. The principles of systematics apply equally well to insects and course content. Smith has been working in Web-based learning since 1997 and teaching online since 1998. She is a Certified Distance Education Professional and Certified Virtual Instructor from the Center for Distance Teaching and Learning at Texas A&M University, as well as a Certified Blackboard Trainer. Smith developed the Center for Web-Based Learning in 1999 and began sharing her knowledge of course development and teaching immediately. She has made over 140 presentations and workshops at local, regional, national, and international conferences. In addition, she has designed and developed over sixty Web-based courses.

Smith has served as an instructional design consultant on numerous Web-based learning federal grants and has facilitated multiple four-day Conquering the Content Workshops, where she guides faculty in the development of their course content and demonstrates the concepts of teaching and learning.

Conquering the Content

Design with Learning in Mind

Learning Goals/Outcomes	
Design with Learning in Mind	Upon completion of this chapter, the faculty member will be able to: • Recognize the need to design the course from students' point of view. • Understand how course content can be altered appropriately for Web-based learning. • Document current course outcomes. • Review two learning styles inventories and the associated study resources.

Learning Resources	
References	• Chickering, A., and Gamson, Z. "Seven Principles for Good Practice in Undergraduate Education." *AAHE Bulletin,* Mar. 1987, pp. 3–6. • Felder, R. "Learning and Teaching Styles in Engineering Education." *Engineering Education,* 1988, *78*(7), 674–481. • Merrill, M. "First Principles of Instruction." *Educational Technology Research and Development,* 2002, *50*(3), 43–59.

Required Resources	• Chapter One *Conquering the Content*
Additional Resources	Learning styles inventories: Complete these two inventories:
	• http://vark-learn.com
	• http://www.engr.ncsu.edu/learningstyles/ilsweb.htm

Learning Activities

Activities for this lesson	Gather all resources related to the course on which you will be working.
	• Complete Form 1 in Appendix A.
	• Complete Form 2A, 2B, and 2C in Appendix A.
	• Complete Form 3 in Appendix A.
	• Complete Form 4 in Appendix A.
	• Complete two learning styles inventories.

Self-Assessment

Check your understanding	In order to be prepared for the lesson evaluation and the following modules, you should have:
	• Gathered course materials to verify these will be available as you revise course.
	• Completed Form 1 in Appendix A.
	• Completed Form 2A, 2B, and 2C in Appendix A.
	• Completed Form 3 in Appendix A.
	• Completed Form 4 in Appendix A.

Lesson Evaluation

Evidence to proceed	• Course materials and completed forms from this chapter will be used in the next several chapters.

As faculty members we usually choose our subject matter because of passion for that topic. The natural world and problem solving intrigue me, therefore I originally trained as a scientist. What is it that made you select your discipline? Perhaps it was a teacher who took a special interest in you, a class that challenged you, some particular lesson that touched you at a sensitive time in your life, or somehow things just clicked when you thought about a certain subject and it all just made sense to you.

My goal with *Conquering the Content* is to allow you to remain that subject matter expert. Therefore, I will give you enough information to understand how learning takes place, how teaching online is different from teaching in the classroom, what you need to do to get your course online, information about course design and organization, and how to avoid some of the common pitfalls encountered as development progresses in Web-based courses. This book presents a practical approach that will lead you through the development of online course content as you proceed through the book. If you follow the system in this book, the course content you develop will be well organized and pedagogically sound with opportunities for active learning. In addition, the content will be formatted for easy updates at any time, and direct uploading into a learning management system.

The plan this book follows is one in which you will look at your course as a whole, select the highest-priority topics for the overall course, and place those items online first. In this way, the fundamentals for the entire course will be established and produced prior to adding anything fancy or flashy to any one topic (referred to here as *modules*). You may not have an award-winning module 1, but you will have the basis of the entire course completed. As an online instructor, I've found the latter is much preferable to the former. *Conquering the Content* provides information to add layers to your course as your skills and experience grow.

Later you may have that award-winning course, but you probably also will have some online teaching experience to make the revisions you'll need for that award. More important, you won't end up as I did in my first semester of teaching online when, way too close to the beginning of the semester, I had an awesome module 1 and nothing for the remainder of the course. Much of what I share with you in this book comes from my own experience of making a multitude of mistakes and finding ways to correct them. I want to help prevent you and others from repeating my time-consuming and frustrating mistakes.

Each chapter ends with a list of action steps and time estimates for these activites that will lead you through development of your course. Appendix B also assists you in planning course development based on the amount of time you have prior to the beginning of your course.

The process described in this book is based on educational principles, adult learning principles, Web-based learning principles, and brain and learning theory. It is not subject matter specific. This process has already proven successful for nursing, biological sciences, physical sciences, humanities, history, composition, literature, psychology, philosophy, speech, technical writing, elementary education, mathematics, computer science, accounting, gerontology, wastewater treatment, sleep deprivation, ethics, psychiatry, communications, pharmacy, and numerous other courses.

Learning in the Twenty-First Century

Just as you want just enough information to put your course online, detailed steps about how to do the things you need to do, pitfalls to avoid, all without a bunch of extraneous explanations or background information, so do students. Think about how you proceed when you go to the Internet to look up information. You undoubtedly search to find:

- The best match for the subject at hand. You don't want to read thirty articles, just find a few of the facts you need and extract those facts yourself.

- Quick-loading information. If you have to wait more than five or ten seconds (or fifteen to twenty, on depending on the speed of your connection) for a page to load, you no doubt abandon that site for a different one.

- Clear, precise information with images to confirm you have identified things correctly or are going about the steps to a new task correctly.

- Checks or verifications along the way in a project so you don't get to the end of a sixteen-step process and find out you did something wrong in step 2. You want to know on step 2 whether you are right before proceeding to step 3.

- Few to no time wasters, which are frustrating and preventable.

Learning online is very different from learning in the classroom, and so what has worked for teaching materials in the past is not going to be suitable for Web-based teaching. This is a rather tough adjustment for most faculty. We usually teach as we were taught, and those teachers taught us the way they had been taught, and so the cycle has gone for many decades or centuries. As Tony Bates, a prominent authority on distance learning points out, "to change is more work. You've got to be trained; you've got to learn new things; you've got to do things that you've never done before" (Awalt, 2007, p. 107).

Today we have powerful tools that have altered the learning environment and offer opportunities to work in new ways. In addition, we are constantly discovering new information about learning and brain research. Moreover, today's students have grown up in a visual environment, and they typically process multiple things at one time. They may simultaneously be searching the Web, listening to music, and talking on the phone. Then we wonder why they can't pay attention when they sit in our course and we lecture to them continuously for fifty minutes.

Advantages to Having a Course Online

I knew students would appreciate the convenience of accessing information on their own schedule, no class attendance requirement, and the ability to review course content and presentations more than the one time they were presented in the classroom. However, after my course was online, I realized additional advantages that I had not anticipated. Some of these advantages were due to advanced preparation of the Web-based course, which had to be complete before the semester began. For example:

- Students in my classroom course also benefit from learning guides being provided to them.

- Students are able to view the materials more than one time.

- Students can hurry through concepts that are familiar to them and go slower through concepts for which they need additional time.

- The Web-based course provided a permanent base from which to update my course since everything was documented and review of contents was more convenient.

- Static content enabled the students to provide more meaningful feedback on aspects and portions of the content that might need an added component.

- I knew for certain what the online students were viewing for magnified images. Whereas when we met in the laboratory, I was unable to check with each student on each microscope slide.

- It was much easier for me to critique my own course materials than to critique a video tape of myself presenting those materials.

- It was easier to incorporate the suggestions from external reviews since they could review the course material on their own time. The Web-based materials provided a target for review that was impersonal compared to critiquing my classroom presentations. Reviewers found it much more comfortable to provide constructive feedback.

How Web-Based Learning Is the Same as Classroom Learning

Think of your favorite teacher from all your years of school—the one who made a lasting impression on you. Using Form 1 in Appendix A, document the qualities that stood out about his or her teaching. (Remember that all forms are in Appendix A.) Typically, a person's favorite teacher is not one who was their easiest teacher, rather perhaps the person provided motivation, inspiration, or practical application. Your students may find these qualities very beneficial as well. The most effective teaching principles have been documented by several studies.

You may be familiar with the classic study by Chickering and Gamson (1987), which established seven principles for undergraduate teaching:

- Encourage faculty-to-student interaction.
- Encourage student-to-student interaction.
- Promote active learning.
- Communicate high expectations.
- Facilitate time on task.
- Provide rich, rapid feedback.
- Respect diverse learning.

These same teaching principles hold true whether you are teaching in the classroom or in a Web-based course. If you are not familiar with these principles, I encourage you to find this classic study online. Among the many other papers based on Chickering and Gamson's original work is Chickering and Ehrmann's "Implementing the Seven Principles: Technology as Lever" (1996), which provides ideas for using the seven principles in a Web-based course.

Another excellent guide for Web-based courses is Merrill's "First Principles of Instruction" (2002). Most effective learning environments are those that are problem based and involve student in four distinct phases of learning:

- Activation of prior experience
- Demonstration of skills
- Application of skills
- Integration of these skills into real-world activities

Instructional design applications based on these principles follow:

- Learning is facilitated when learners are engaged in solving real-world problems.
- Learning is facilitated when existing knowledge is activated as a foundation for new knowledge.
- Learning is facilitated when new knowledge is demonstrated to the learner.
- Learning is facilitated when applied by the learner.
- Learning is facilitated when integrated into the learner's world.

No one would expect an athlete or a musician to perform without hours of practice. Yet much instruction seems to assume that when it comes to cognitive skills, such practice is unnecessary. Merrill (2002) notes that "appropriate practice is the single most neglected aspect of effective instruction" (p. 43).

Knowledge and skill are soon forgotten if they are not made part of the learner's life beyond instruction. Learners need the opportunity to reflect on, defend, and share what they have learned if it is to become part of their available repertoire (Merrill, 2002).

The principles documented by Chickering and Gamson and by Merrill are important to keep in mind when it comes time to develop the learning guides for your online course.

Learning Styles

Web-based learners have a variety of learning styles, just as classroom students do. It can be enlightening for your students to complete a learning styles inventory. You might direct them to these two: VARK Learning Styles Inventory (http://www .vark-learn.com) or Felder's Inventory (http://www.engr.ncsu.edu/learningstyles/ ilsweb.html).

The Felder (1993) inventory addresses global and sequential information processing. Those individuals who process information globally are skilled at viewing issues via a picture view. Those who process sequentially usually proceed step-wise through the information considering individual details prior to understanding the big picture. The Web site provides several ways to help faculty meet different learning styles. In particular, faculty seldom give the big picture of what we are teaching prior to delving into the details. Nevertheless, it is important for students who are global learners that we present the global picture at the beginning (just as I outlined in the Preface what this book is about) and connect what the students are about to learn with some subjects with which they are already familiar. This process allows students to frame the new knowledge in its proper context.

Sheila Tobias's research on students who set out to be science majors and changed their major after the first year highlights the issues between sequential and global information processing. Science courses at the time she did her research were frequently taught sequentially, without providing a global overview. Tobias found that the overwhelming number of those who changed their major were global learners (Tobias, 1991).

Finding out about learning styles has changed the way I teach. I thought everyone learns by taking notes and reorganizing the information into different configurations until they know and understand it from several different angles.

That my way of learning is not everyone's approach was very eye-opening for me. I learned this from a student in one of my classroom courses who was failing the lab exams. Spelling counted in these exams, since in anatomy, the change of one letter in a word can give it a totally different meaning. She also could not pronounce the words correctly, and I was continually trying to help her get the pronunciations correct. We came up with a solution: I recorded the lab words on tape for her. I repeated each word slowly three times before I moved to the next one. Once I finished the list that way, I went back through the entire list saying each word one time and asking her to repeat the word after me, this time pausing long enough on the tape for her to do so. On the next lab exam, she earned a 98 percent. She and I both were elated, and I made a tape for her for each of the remaining exams. Perhaps you are thinking, "Yes, but that takes too much time!" It does take time, but in the whole scheme of things, those few minutes I spent each week were well worth my time to accommodate her learning style.

Look back at the information you wrote in Form 1 about your favorite teacher. Did this person make a special effort to relate to the students? Did the person take a special interest in you? Many times that is the case. Most of us decided to teach so that we could make a difference in people's lives. But when the opportunity arises, sometimes we tend to shrink back because of time constraints. Let us not rob ourselves of the rewards of our profession for fear of investing time in our students and in creating learning opportunities for them. Most of us are successful because someone took the time to take a special interest in us and invest extra time in our lives.

If you haven't already done so, complete the VARK learning styles inventory (http:/www.vark-learn.com) and record your scores here:

Visual: _____

Auditory: _____

Read/Write: _____

Kinesthetic: _____

Predominant style: _____

Knowing our predominant style is important because we tend to teach in ways that favor it. Instead, we need to strive to present information in ways that are useful to all learning styles.

One of the biggest advantages to having your students complete learning skills inventories is that following submission of the questionnaire, students are presented with access to many practical suggestions for studying. These learning styles inventories provide an entry point for students to consider the techniques from a neutral source and in a way that does not imply they don't know something; rather they learn study techniques appropriate for their specific strengths. It is critical that students learn how to study, and any tool that facilitates this can prove the key to reaching our students.

Now take the Felder Inventory, (http://www.engr.ncsu.edu/learningstyles/ilsweb.html) and record your scores here:

Place numerical score in the first blank and letter identification in second blank.

Perceiving versus Intuitive _____   Letter _____

Visual versus Auditory _____   Letter _____

Inductive versus Deductive _____   Letter _____

Active versus Reflective _____   Letter _____

Sequential versus Global _____   Letter _____

Many teachers are sequential perceivers, meaning that they need information to come in through the five senses and in a sequential manner. Intuitive learners learn in fits and starts. They may get the answer, but cannot explain where or how they got the answer. At times these individuals can be accused of cheating because they cannot identify the steps to working out the math problem, even though they know the correct answer. It takes them a while to discern how they arrive at what it is they know.

It is very important that you know the learning styles of your students in order to be able to work with them in your course. In Chapter Three when we discuss assessment and the process of grading throughout the semester, and in particular when it comes to the early and intermediate steps of projects, intuitive learners may have great difficulties. In addition, your teaching style may or may not be compatible with all of your students' learning styles.

Felder (1988) defines teaching style in terms of answers to five questions:

1. What types of information does the instructor emphasize?

2. What mode of presentation is stressed?

3. How is the presentation organized?

4. What mode of student participation is facilitated by the presentation?

5. What type of perspective is provided on the information presented?

These questions are important to consider when creating learning materials for your students.

Form 11 provides a place for you to record your students' learning styles. Using this when you speak to your students about studying will give you an opportunity to better assist or better direct them to appropriate resources. In addition, the data collected from these forms may highlight the need for additional resources for portions of your course to address specific learning styles. For example, if a number of students who are visual learners have questions about a particular portion of the content, this could signal that additional visual or graphical aids on this content will prove beneficial.

Think "Learning," Not "Teaching"

We typically think of our courses as what we will teach. Instead, if you alter your thinking to that of the students in your course and think, "What do students need to learn?" this change of perspective will help the design process tremendously. One of the mistakes faculty make (often unconsciously) is to add more work to a Web-based course than to a classroom course. Accrediting agencies expect Web-based courses to be equivalent to classroom courses, asking neither more nor less of students in those courses than of students in a classroom course. The learning strategies may be different, but the content covered and learning outcomes should be the same.

The Online Student's Environment

Just as it was best for me to write this book fully accepting the fact that you will not have the opportunity to place your entire Web-based course online all at once, it is best for you to develop your course fully accepting that your students will not have uninterrupted time to work on your Web-based course. It would be ideal if they had a protected hour to work on the course when nothing else was happening, but how many of us have blocks of time with no interruptions? We need to plan with an understanding that students will have interruptions. If they do not, all the better, but telling them they need to put aside a specific time to work on your course and commit to that time is like expecting students to have questions for you only during your office hours.

Rather than being surrounded by a room full of other students who are focused on your subject matter for a period of time, an online student may be surrounded by any number of circumstances at home. Crying babies have no concern for class time; if they are in distress, now is the time for action. By the same token, ringing phones, toddlers, meal preparations, carpools, work, and other duties often require that students interrupt their Web-based learning time. Do not underestimate the distractions that a student may be dealing with at home. These distractions will have an effect on their concentration levels for Web-based courses.

How Web-Based Learning Is Different from Classroom Learning

One of the most notable differences between the classroom and the Web-based environment is just that: the environment. First, you aren't standing at the front of the room ready to dispense the knowledge to the students. In addition, there aren't twenty to four hundred other people surrounding the student, all with a dedicated fifty minutes devoted solely to the subject matter.

Altered Learning Environment

In the classroom when you give encouraging words to one student, you are simultaneously giving positive feedback to all the students. But online students never hear these words to other students. Nor do they hear you say "good morning" and see a smile from you each class period. None of those cues are available to students in Web-based courses. Instead, for online students, everything becomes verbal; it takes lots of verbal positive reinforcement to replace all those visual cues that are not happening.

It is crucial for your students' benefit and for your own self-preservation that your course be designed in such a way that it creates a clear pathway of learning for the students. The most frequent criticism I hear about Web-based courses is how confusing the course is or how unclear it is to find the proper path within the course.

For a classroom course, you and the students go into the classroom and shut the door. There is almost no record of what is said in that classroom except for the notes that students take. In a Web-based course, in contrast, there is a visible, archived record of what you have presented for the class. This is more like publishing an article or a chapter in a book than teaching a class. Your course materials are now representing not only you but also your department and your institution. Peer review thus becomes a vitally important part of your course. Typographical errors in your course materials, for example, reflect poorly on you, your department, and your institution.

The design of the online course becomes much more important than in a classroom. You'll need to make a few alterations in your course materials in order to accomplish the same learning outcomes in a very different environment. And as you do, you will have numerous opportunities for teaching in more effective ways.

When I thought in terms of my biology lab, I had the freedom not to worry about spending time getting to twenty-five students and telling each of them, "No, that is not the *Amoeba*; that is a speck of dust on the cover slip." "No, that is not *Plasmodium*; that is the pointer in the eyepiece."

Learner-Centered Environment

The Web-based environment allows repetition of content. Some students may need to hear a presentation several times in order to be able to absorb it. If the student is willing to invest that amount of time, why should he or she not be able to have that option available? In classroom courses, repeating sections of content usually is not a reasonable option. When content is available in a Web-based course, repetition of information is possible.

The learner-centered environment of an online course has a number of facets:

- *Self-selected.* That students choose when to come into the course and work on the subject matter adds a distinct psychological advantage: they are mentally prepared because they chose to work on the course materials. Even if it's to avoid something else they don't want to do (laundry, working in someone else's course), they've chosen to come to class. In a classroom course, in contrast, the students are required to come to class at a specific time. Even if they originally selected this schedule themselves, who says that on a given Wednesday at 10:00 A.M., it is agreeable for them to be there? By the way, you as a faculty member get to self-select the moment you go to class in a Web-based course too.
- *Time.* Students may work at the time of day when they are at their best. You may be at your best in the morning; if so, you can develop your course in the morning. Some students may be at their best at 11:00 P.M. and "come to class" then. Another student can come to class at 2:00 A.M. With everyone working at their optimum time of the day, both the course and the participation in the course are more likely to be the best effort possible.

- *Place.* Students can choose a place where they can concentrate well and at their convenience. A student who must travel for work or vacation can keep coming to class no matter where he or she is. This means that students can keep up with course work much better than students in the classroom, who if they have a conflict at, say, 10:00 on Monday, totally miss whatever happens in class. In a Web-based course, the attitude is, "Oh, don't worry. Do it later."

- *Pace.* Web-based learning students can move quickly through parts they understand, go slowly through parts they don't understand, and repeat sections as needed. Faculty members have always had the difficulty of not reaching all the students. Some students are left behind, while others aren't challenged enough. With a Web-based course, students can take care of this for themselves. And because materials are already online, there is no extra effort required by the faculty member to meet individual students' needs.

- *Around-the-clock access.* Students can access the course content when you are not available. In classroom courses, access to information is typically available during class time and during the faculty member's office hours. With content and other course materials online, this information is available around the clock.

The Student's Role

Students in a Web-based course are more responsible than those in a classroom course for seeking out knowledge. There is no longer a person standing at the front of the room to guide the student through a lesson for an hour. Online students need enough discipline to come to class by logging in and then working through the content. This is placing more responsibility on the student to begin with. In addition, there is no one there saying, "Class is over at 10 to the hour; you don't leave until then."

The greater responsibility on the student is another reason that directions and the pathway for progress through the course must be abundantly clear to students: There is an increased need for them to communicate with each other. Learning guides, discussed later in this book, can help facilitate this communication.

Because of these differences in the environment, course content requires these components:

- Short, directed learning segments—Chunk-ability
- Ability to repeat and review content—Repeat-ability

- Ability to stop and resume without having to start all over—Pause-ability

- Clear, direct instructions—Understand-ability

We'll talk more about these issues as you develop your content presentations.

The Faculty Member's Role

One of the changes in the faculty role is the distinction between development and design activities, and facilitation and teaching activities in courses. You may find yourself developing a course you do not end up teaching or teaching a course you did not develop. This is becoming more and more common as institutions begin to rely on adjunct teaching staff for Web-based teaching. Whether that is your situation or not, development and facilitation are independent activities in Web-based courses. Development and design activities are best accomplished and completed prior to the beginning of the semester, so that the semester may be spent on the facilitation and teaching aspects of the course.

There is a tremendous advantage to placing teaching materials into usable enduring materials. Once the course units or modules have been developed, time can be spent on revisions. The instructor is then free to interact with participants in the course. After you have taught your course online one time, you can build from the foundation you have created. Your starting point will be much higher than it was when you began, so you will be able to stand on your own shoulders, so to speak, and build from a higher foundation. Your course becomes stronger and more robust each time you teach it.

Course Development and Design The design and development of the course, rather than the facilitation and teaching of the course, is where the transfer of knowledge takes place. In a classroom course, we typically think of teaching as dispensing knowledge, but today, knowledge is readily available (for example, over the Internet), so faculty are no longer the keepers of the knowledge. Instead faculty now explain that information, explore how to make connections with it, decipher what is most important, explain how it matters to everyday life, and so forth. Dispensing knowledge is something a machine can do, and faculty are much more talented and useful than any machine. Our role now is to make sure that information is presented in a way that is relevant, understandable, memorable, and useful to the students.

I was working with a faculty member who was developing a Web-based course. He was in a large group of mixed subject matter experts, so I was speaking in general terms. It turned out that his course was for remedial reading students. It was a blended course, and therefore not completely Web based, but some customization was in order. We knew that these students have some difficulties, and expecting them to learn to read by posting lots of course documents was a definite stretch. This goes back to the point that Web-based courses have to be planned from the beginning. One of the ways that students learn to read is by hearing others read out loud and by reading out loud themselves, so I suggested some ways to incorporate audio files and assignments in which the students would read out loud and turn in those readings. There are ways to teach most subjects online, but you have to be thoughtful about the way courses are planned.

Course Facilitation and Teaching As facilitators and teachers in Web-based courses, we lead students rather than dispense knowledge to them. We become the bridge between students and content rather than the source of the content. It is a perhaps subtle change but nevertheless important because it means taking on different responsibilities.

A faculty member who is acting as the sage is reaping the benefits of working with, structuring, and communicating the content. One goal in designing effective and efficient learning environments is for students to work as intensively with the content. Strategies that support this shift in perspective include having the students moderate discussion forums, prepare concept summaries and examples for other students, and assume greater responsibility as frontline moderators for the course (Boettcher, 2007).

Design features incorporated in this system of course development and the learning guide will create an environment in which students are confident of their pathway, and the only challenge is the course content, not the navigation of the course or figuring out what must be done in order to complete the course. This focus on students when designing the course will free you up to spend the semester teaching and interacting with the students in regard to the content rather than answering questions about course navigation or specific directions about assignments.

Course logistics questions detract from the true reason faculty are available for their students: for students to learn information they cannot get from any other source. A properly designed and developed course should trigger very few logistical questions during the semester, so your time can be spent on interacting with students, not developing or designing your course.

Appendix D provides a list of design and development tasks.

Advanced Planning

Your students are extremely busy individuals and need to be able to plan their lives in advance. One way I helped my students was to commit to test dates at the beginning of the semester so they could arrange work schedules, babysitters, and other help. I would not change test dates on them. If I had to be flexible about something, I might change the amount of material covered on the exam but not the date. This commitment to the students and my respect for them set a tone of professional courtesy in the course that ends up working to everyone's advantage.

For now, it will be helpful to document what is currently taking place in the course you'd like to work with as we work through *Conquering the Content*. The action steps that follow will help you proceed to Chapter Two, which addresses making sure course materials are in a format that can be ready to be easily updated.

Action Steps

You should have already completed the learning styles inventories and recorded your results.

Step 1

Select one course to develop as you work through this book. You may have more than one you need to complete, but for now, choose only one. Preferably this course will be taught a semester or two in the future so you will have some time to work through this book.

Complete Form 1 in Appendix A by reflecting on former teachers and the qualities they possessed to become your favorite teacher. Your students will also appreciate these same qualities in you.

Time estimate: 5 minutes

Step 2

Gather all materials for the entire semester in one place for the Web-based course you will be developing: textbooks, lecture notes, journal articles, electronic files, assignments, and so on. This step will be more time-consuming for some individuals than for others. The large time variance is based on the fact that some faculty will have their materials already assembled at their fingertips, while other faculty may have to spend substantial time collecting course lecture notes, reference articles, and other course materials which may not already be assembled in one place.

Time estimate: 5 minutes to 15 hours

Step 3

Document the way the course is currently organized. How do you give grades? Do you have a series of quizzes? Projects? Exams? Papers? Whatever you normally do in the classroom, put that information on Forms 2A, 2B, and 2C.

Time estimate: 20 minutes

Step 4

Complete Form 3 on course revisions.

Time estimate: 12 minutes

Step 5

Using your favorite search engine, search for online course content in your subject matter area. The following sites will prove useful:

- World Lecture Hall, http://web.austin.utexas.edu/wlh/

  Open to faculty, developers, and students alike, World Lecture Hall publishes links to pages created by educators worldwide who produce Web-based course materials in any language. While some courses are delivered entirely over the Internet, others are designed for students in residence. Many fall somewhere in between. In all cases, they can be visited by anyone interested in Web-based courses.

- Merlot, www.merlot.org/

  Multimedia Education Resource for Learning and Online Teaching (MERLOT) provides peer-reviewed online teaching and learning materials. Professionals are encouraged to share advice and expertise about education with expert colleagues.

- MIT OpenCourseWare, http://ocw.mit.edu

  In its ongoing commitment to advancing education and discovery through knowledge open to everyone, Massachusetts Institute of Technology (MIT) OpenCourseWare provides free lecture notes, exams, and other resources from over 1,800 courses from MIT's entire curriculum.

- Lolaexchange, www.lolaexchange.org/

  Sponsored by Wesleyan University, Lolaexchange contains materials for use across the curriculum with an emphasis on modules for information literacy. LoLa facilitates the exchange of information pertaining to high-quality learning objects.

- MedEdPORTAL, www.aamc.org/mededportal

  A service of the Association of American Medical Colleges, MedEdPORTAL is an evolving resource. Educators and students from around the world are encouraged to explore free peer-reviewed materials.

You can place in the search box the name of the subject you are interested in plus the term "course" or "course content." Get a sense of how content is presented in the areas you search. Observe the things you like or don't like about each. Spend some time developing an eye for what seems logical and easy to follow versus courses or materials that are less organized or not as easy to grasp. You may use the Ideas for Application pages at the end of the book to record design elements that appeal to you.

Time estimate: 30 minutes to 2 hours

Step 6

Document on Form 4 the current sequence of chapters in your course. Convert these chapter numbers to the name of the topic covered in each chapter. These topics will now become the *modules* for your course. (Hereafter I will refer to them as modules.)

Time estimate: 7 to 15 minutes

Design with the Future in Mind

Learning Goals/Outcomes	

Design with the Future in Mind	Upon completion of this chapter, the faculty member will be able to:
	• Develop a Web-based course which will accommodate the following changes without any additional reformatting:
	  • Flexibility of teaching schedules (fifteen-week term, four-week term, ten-week term, etc.)
	  • Revisions to textbooks
	  • Rapid updates to content
	  • Addition of components to the course

Learning Resources	
Required resources *Additional resources*	• Chapter 2 *Conquering the Content* • None

Learning Activities	
Activities for this lesson	• Complete Form 5 in Appendix A. • Complete Form 6 in Appendix A. • Complete Form 7 in Appendix A.

Self-Assessment	
Check your understanding	• Complete learning activities to begin developing flexible, updatable course materials.

Lesson Evaluation	
"Graded" assessments or evidence to proceed	• These forms will be used to further create content in subsequent chapters.

I'd like to think that every Web-based course has ample development time, a graphic artist, an instructional designer, a Flash developer, a peer review team, a production staff, a pilot test with students, and time for redevelopment following those activities. However, most of us are essentially on our own to design, develop, and produce our Web-based courses. So we do indeed have some things to conquer.

It's Okay to Be Uncomfortable

Faculty members are experts in their subject matter, and if you have many years of teaching experience, you most likely feel comfortable in the classroom. Many faculty thrive on the experience of sharing what they know with others. Often they have become accustomed to sharing their knowledge with others in a classroom setting. If faculty are suddenly asked to alter those surroundings and place a course online, that leads to some major adjustments.

First, rather than being the expert, you find yourself in unfamiliar surroundings. You might think, "I don't know how to put my course online, and I don't have time to put my course online." Nevertheless, put your mind at ease; you are *supposed* to feel uncomfortable about this and unsure about what you are doing. That is natural the first time you do something. It might feel uncomfortable even for a few semesters. It is okay to do things scared.

All of us who have put a course online did so the first time not really knowing what we were doing. In fact this discomfort may actually be an advantage according to Weimer (2002): "When we opt for change that is not comfortable and is entirely out of the ordinary for us, we open ourselves to teaching as a learning experience, a point of personal development" (p. 188). You are still going to be the subject matter expert; you may not be the technical expert, but honestly, do you really want to be? It is expected that you will ask for help on technical matters; you are not compromising your expertise.

I work in a medical facility where there are renowned surgeons and physicians. There is no question that some of these physicians are prestigious individuals in their specialty. However, they may not know as much about Web-based learning as I do. Does that call their expertise into question? Absolutely not. They ask me questions about Web-based learning, but I probably don't even know enough to have the right words to ask questions about their specialties. Do not feel your position as a subject matter expert is being compromised by this new experience. You know who you are, and so does everyone else. It's not an issue.

Of course, you are going to have questions about Web-based learning and the course management system; that is a given. But you don't have time to learn everything there is to know about all of it, only what you need to know in order to teach your course. Pick the brains of others around you; most people love to share information.

The Future Will Be Here Sooner Than You Think

Most courses need to be updated soon after being produced; therefore, it is best to have a course design from the beginning that accommodates updates. The course design described in this book is strategically planned so that the design and organization of documents and placement of certain aspects of the course are formatted for course updates to be streamlined and accomplished in a systematic way.

Perhaps you are now teaching a course that meets only in the fall, and you have no plans to change that schedule. Nevertheless, with the rapidly changing e-learning environment, it is difficult to anticipate exactly what changes will take place in the next few years. Therefore, by following the system in this book, you will be ready when the need arises for you to teach the course in a five-week summer term, or a four-week midwinter course, or any other scheduling options that might arise. We will be naming content based on modules rather than weeks. Also, book and chapter number references will be confined to a particular place (learning guides) so that tracking down those references throughout the many pages of course information is unnecessary.

In addition, this course design system will prepare you for the new edition of the textbook you use. As educators, we do not want to place ourselves in the position that our course materials are in such great shape that we do not want to update them or that it is too much trouble to update them. As I created my first Web-based course, I realized how much work I was putting into it and knew I had to make it easy to update; starting from scratch was going to be more than I was prepared to tackle in the near future. Content in this system is named and labeled in a logical and retrievable manner and is in segments short enough that when changes are needed, large portions of the course do not have to be recreated.

In addition to textbook and information updates, sometimes a rapid response time is extremely important when updates to content are needed. In a project I was involved with, there was a need to release content revisions to medical students concerning the switch in position on hormone replacement therapy, and to do so quickly. We needed to be able to update the Web-based course in one week. The majority of that time was spent on getting the content developed; updating the course was accomplished in minutes. Fortunately, the design of the course allowed the updates to be added easily. Following this design system will allow you to do the same.

This system will also accommodate adding components to the course progressively as you teach. The majority of teachers are constantly monitoring and adjusting, and it is no different in a Web-based course. After you have taught your Web-based course the first time, you will find parts you'd like to alter based on your experience and student feedback. This system makes editing and adding improvements to your course easy.

Creating the Outline

It is time to make final decisions about the module titles and their sequence. You may normally cover ten to twenty-five or more major segments or sections in your course. We will designate each of these as a *module* and hereafter use that name. From Form 4, review, revise, and verify module titles for your new Web-based course. Record your results on Form 5. Remember, all forms are in Appendix A.

Each module will have a selected number of competencies or outcomes. I recommend clumping the competencies into five to seven per module. I go into the reasoning for this in Chapter Five, but basically it is so that students can group the knowledge into manageable segments and more easily retrieve that information.

Please refer to Table 2.1 for an overview of the entire content organization.

Record the modules on Form 6. Then divide (or group) the elements of each module into five to seven outcomes or competencies, and record these in the right-hand column of Form 6. You can further divide these into major points or to create an additional grouping for very complex material divide the competencies first into subtopics and then into major points. Form 8 provides a place to drill down to the major point level, but I find many people like to have a shorter outline of the big picture, which Form 6 provides. Notice the major points are a subdivision of the competencies or outcomes on Form 6.

How inclusive should a competency be? It is most manageable if it is substantial enough that you'd like to have an assignment on the competency. For example, in an English course, the instructor may have the students write ten short papers throughout the semester, so she might choose to organize the course based on those ten papers. A history instructor might have twenty quizzes throughout the semester and design the competencies based on those quizzes. Or use your learning guide (see Form 9 as modeled at the front of each chapter of *Conquering the Content*) as your guide. If the learning segment is not substantial enough to warrant the information found on a learning guide (described in the next section), then perhaps that segment would benefit from being combined with another segment.

Keep in mind one of Chickering and Gamson's principles of good teaching: frequent feedback. If you typically use just a midterm and final exam, this is a good opportunity to incorporate more frequent assessments so students will have a better opportunity to improve their performance based on early intervention.

The Learning Guide

The learning guide serves as a one-page overview of the learning module and is the key to easy updates for your course. It is also the guide for developing the course and prioritizing portions of it to work on first. In addition, the learning guides will make the course expectations clear and organized for your students. It appears to be a lot of work to develop the learning guides, and it is. But once you

Table 2.1. Content Organization

Course	Module	Competency	Major Points
Biology	1	1	1 2 3 4 5 6 7
		2	1 2 3 4 5 6 7
		3	1 2 3 4 5 6 7
		4	1 2 3 4 5 6 7
		5	1 2 3 4 5 6 7
		6	1 2 3 4 5 6 7
		7	1 2 3 4 5 6 7

develop it for your course, you will have an easy-to-follow map and a checklist of exactly what you need to do to develop the remainder of that course. In addition, your students will have a checklist for what they need to do to complete each module in the course. This gives you an automatic time savings during the semester because students will not bombard you with procedural questions since the procedures are already spelled out.

The payoff for developing these learning guides is huge. You don't have to call it a learning guide or use the format I do. You can create something that fits your own style. However you do it, it creates a map of what each module includes and is beneficial for both you and your students.

Learning Guide Purposes

There are two main purposes for a learning guide.

The first is course development. The learning guide is a tool to help create an outline for the course. I suggest that you develop one for each module in the course and do so before developing any portion of the course itself. These learning guides then serve as a course development guide, a guide for gathering resources, and a foundation from which to set priorities for course development.

The second purpose is as a student learning guide. The learning guide is a printable resource that guides students' learning online and offline. It also serves as a checklist for students so they will be assured their work is complete when they finish all of the items on guide.

Learning Guide Principles

One of the crucial elements of keeping your course easy to update is *never* to embed textbook page numbers or chapter references within course content, quizzes, assignments, discussions, feedback, or any other portion of the course. Textbook page numbers and chapter references should appear *only* on the learning guides. The reason is that when the textbook is revised, you will know exactly where to go in order to update the chapter and page references if the learning guide is the only place you have placed those references. Otherwise you might have to search through hundreds (or thousands) of pages of content, quiz questions, or question feedback for chapter and page references in order to update those.

Another important principle is that you must take a holistic look at the course, stepping back from the fall semester/spring semester/summer term way of thinking.

This can be a difficult step for faculty. Many of us think in terms of weeks of the semester or "from now until spring break, I normally do this." I even had an instructor tell me once that she could not teach a class on Tuesdays and Thursdays because she'd always taught it on Mondays, Wednesdays, and Fridays; all her lectures and assignments were divided up that way, and it would be too hard to alter it all. We sometimes lock ourselves into a routine and forget to take a look at the knowledge as a whole rather than its division into class meetings. Instead, overall course structure should be independent of time and of book chapter.

Online courses are best designed so that they may be taught regardless of the time frame in which they are offered—Not week 1 and week 2, for example, but module 1 and module 2. We need to look at the information and subject that we teach, not the time frame. In the future, who knows if we will still be offering fifteen-week semesters? What if we decide to allow students to concentrate on one subject at a time and saturate themselves in that one course until they've completed the requirements in a reduced time frame and then move to the next course? We want to be ready for all that.

Online courses are also independent of book chapters. If we write the course according to a particular textbook, we'll have to revamp the entire course as soon as the book is revised. We tend to teach the same topics regardless of which edition of the text is used.

In this book, I use topics or module numbers rather than chapter headings to name portions of the course, so when the chapter numbers or sequences change, the course does not need to be reorganized.

It will help you stay organized if you keep an electronic copy of all the folders offline that you will have online in your course. I prefer to edit offline, so I keep a clean copy of my documents in a folder on my hard drive or other storage device. I edit offline and then re-upload that file and overwrite the previous version of the file in my Web-based course. All of the links are still in place, and overwriting the file is the only thing I have to do. Also, with this plan, I have all of my content on my own computer and also backed up on a storage device.

Elements of the Learning Guide

The next chapter goes into detail about developing learning guides. Here is a brief introduction to the elements of the learning guide:

- Identification of modules
- Learning goals/outcomes
- Learning Resources
  - Required resources
  - Additional resources
- Learning Activities
- Self-assessment
- Lesson evaluation

The Modules

Use Form 4 to convert your textbook chapter numbers into topics corresponding with the topics you documented on Form 4, which also gives you an example to follow.

It is now time to gather the resources you will be using in each module. At this point you will need to have made a final decision on the titles for each of your modules. (In the next chapter, we begin to build the elements of the learning guide.)

File Systems

Establishing a file system for your course is a good idea. And since you'll be working on and saving learning guides, it is beneficial to develop that structure before creating the files. The following method has proven helpful for those developing Web-based courses to facilitate long-term storage and retrieval of files.

Naming Schemes Since the topics you teach typically don't change even if the chapter numbers with a new textbook do, it is helpful to use a combination of topic names and module numbers to identify your content. Students won't know whether red blood cells are first or fourth, but you probably will. So "Module 01, Red Blood Cells" is informative enough for everyone to understand what this module is and where it goes in the learning sequence. This labeling becomes critical because it will affect everything about your modules—for example:

- Folders
- Files

- Quiz question names
- Content file names
- Discussion topic names
- Discussion question names
- Assignment titles
- Quiz titles names
- Small group discussion titles
- Presentation files
- Audio files

The list of files you will need to name will be quite long, so using a consistent naming scheme is essential.

Folder and File Structures The correct organization of files will make it easy to update courses. There may be some specific requirements for naming or organizing courses at your institution. But in the absence of those, here is a system I've found useful:

- Make a folder for each module, using leading zeros to number the modules below the number 10 (otherwise they won't sort correctly alphanumerically): Module01, Module02, and so on.
- At some point you may need to make a subfolder for each of the components of the learning guide for which you have multiple files. Label these with the topic name plus the module number. For example, a content subfolder for Module01 becomes ContentM01, and a subfolder for learning resources for Module 01 becomes LearningResourcesM01. Therefore the path for content is Module01/ContentM01, and for learning resources it's Module01/Learning ResourcesM01, or M01LR01.
- Use a consistent naming scheme for files; for example, LGM01 refers to learning guide Module 01.

Managing Course Structure

You will create a system of folders both online and offline that match up and reflect the course structure. This generic system will work regardless of the course being taught or the person working with the course. It will make just as much sense to a clerical assistant as it does to you. The organizational scheme will work regardless of which course you are teaching.

The idea of keeping the same folder and file structure online and offline is that you will always edit offline. Keep a clean copy of your online files offline, so that you will edit in an environment with which you are familiar (MSWord, SoftChalk, FrontPage, DreamWeaver, or any other html editor you may be using) and then convert to html (if necessary) and upload the materials to your learning management system.

Whenever you need to make additional changes, go back to your offline files, edit again, save again *using the same name as before,* and re-upload, rewriting over the existing file in your course management system. All links then still remain in place.

I've had a few people tell me this file folder structure and naming scheme system was the most helpful thing they've done for themselves. It is amazing how a little organization can simplify tasks.

Now that the course organization is in place, in the next chapter we concentrate on developing appropriate assessment and evaluation methods.

Action Steps

You will be producing all content offline prior to *ever* placing any content online.

Step 7

Use Form 5, Course Outline, to identify the major divisions in the course by module.

Time estimate: 30 minutes to 1 hour

Step 8

On your computer's hard drive or the place you are going to store your files, make a folder for one module; label it M01.

Time estimate: 2 minutes

Step 9

Inside the folder labeled M01 make a subfolder for that module for each of the components of the learning guide for which you will have multiple files—for example:

- ContentM01
- LearningResourcesM01
- AssignmentsM01

Again, label them each so you will know they belong to Module01. Place all folders on your computer's hard drive or the place you are going to store your files.

Time estimate: 5 minutes

Step 10

Copy the folder and subfolder structure you just created, and paste it into the main course folder enough times to have a set of folders and subfolders for each of your modules. Rename the new folders according to the module number. Use leading zeros and number the folders for modules below the number 10 (for example, Module01, Module02). These will be the names seen in the filing system, but it is more helpful to use topic names in the areas where students are able to view the names (this will be inside the learning management system).

Time estimate: 15 minutes

Step 11

Use Form 6 to document five to seven major competencies for each module. As you create content documents, use a consistent naming scheme for naming files—for example, learning guide module 01 is LGM01.

Step 12

Select five to seven major points within which to organize the content for each competency, and record these on Form 8, The students will be able to remember the content better if it is arranged into groupings or categories of information. This may require you to prioritize the information for this competency and use the highest priority items at this time. Repeat this step for each of the modules for your course.

Time estimate: 2–5 hours

CHAPTER

3

Design with Assessment in Mind

Learning Goals/Outcomes	
Development of learning guides	Upon completion of this chapter, the faculty member will:
	• Develop assessment measures for lessons.
	• Choose authentic assessments as often as possible.
	• Be aware of the limitations of objective tests.
	• Include formative assessment during course.
	• Brainstorm new ways to teach course outcomes.
	• Develop new teaching options not limited to the classroom.

Learning Resources	
Required resources *Additional resources*	• Chapter 3 *Conquering the Content*
	• Appendix C—AAHE Principles of Good Practice for Assessing Student Learning, 2003.
	• Comeaux, P. *Assessing Online Learning.* San Francisco: Jossey-Bass, 2005.
	• Finkelstein, J. *Learning in Real Time: Synchronous Teaching and Learning Online.* San Francisco: Jossey-Bass, 2006.
	• Walvoord, B. E., and Anderson, V. A. *Effective Grading: A Tool for Learning and Assessment.* San Francisco: Jossey-Bass, 1998.

Learning Activities	
Activities for this lesson	• Develop assessment plan for each topic using Form 7. • Determine point values and grading scheme for assessment measures.

Self-Assessment	
Check your understanding	• Ability to develop authentic assessments • Ability to include formative assessment

Lesson Evaluation	
"Graded" assessments or evidence to proceed	• Assessment measures will complete graded assessment or evidence to proceed portion of learning guide.

One of Chickering and Gamson's teaching principles (1987), "Give rich and rapid feedback," tells us that we need to give both formative (along the way, assist with determining learning structures) assessments and summative assessments (those that evaluate the learning of the student). If the assessments are opportunities for students to learn, then we are using every opportunity to refine their knowledge as well as evaluate and refine our course. I refer to formative assessments as assessments and summative assessments as evaluations. One exercise may provide both assessment and evaluation information, but in general I will separate the two in this chapter.

Merrill's premise (2002) that practice with an opportunity to make mistakes, evaluate performance, and correct those mistakes is one of the best ways to learn also directs us toward formative assessments with opportunities for feedback and the opportunity to improve performance.

Both Chickering and Gamson (1987) and Merrill (2002) point toward self-assessment opportunities for students. It is important that students have the opportunity to verify their own learning and remediate themselves prior to a graded evaluation. In addition, functional and authentic assessments are becoming much more commonplace. The American Association of Higher Education Assessment Forum has established assessment principles that are found in Appendix C in this book.

An additional function of assessment and evaluation in an online course is to provide the faculty member with information about students' understanding of the concepts. There are many ways in the classroom to see in students' faces whether they got the point just made; blank stares, for example, are a sign that they didn't understand a word of what was just presented. As instructors, we have to find a way to communicate this same information back to online students. It is important to build in feedback mechanisms so you have a sense of when additional explanations or the opportunity to quicken the pace of the content are needed.

Self-Assessment

Moreno (2004) found that explanatory feedback promotes higher scores and reduces cognitive load compared to corrective feedback. It is thus better to tell students why an answer is correct or incorrect rather than just that it is right or wrong. At the moment of incorrect thinking, you can correct their thinking and explain why it is this way or that.

Incorporate retesting and lots of practice with this concept. Good techniques to do this are self-tests, tests without scores, and scores that do not count. Some faculty members allow students to have unlimited practice on quizzes and record only the highest score. Other faculty members take an average of all scores so that students have some responsibility for good performance the first time taking the quiz. And still others record the first score as a grade, but then allow students to continue to take the quiz as practice in preparation for later assessments. A final option is to record the last score. Your choice depends on your goal for quizzes or tests and your philosophy about their function within the entirety of your course.

In a medical terminology course I taught, I encouraged the students to take the weekly quizzes five times (there were alternate questions on the quizzes, so students did not get the same quiz each time), and I recorded only the highest score. I did this for two reasons. I knew that the more frequently they practiced and the more repetition they had with the terms, the better off they would be when it came to the major test. In addition, I did not want any of the students to make a perfect grade on the first or second attempt and be afraid of taking the quiz again for practice for fear of messing up their perfect score.

That is what I thought worked best in my situation, but other people choose other ways of managing quizzes. You have to customize all of these things to fit your teaching style, students, subject matter, and institutional environment.

Authentic Assessments

It is increasingly important to use student assessments that fit real-world circumstances. Especially with nontraditional-age students who have many life experiences to share, it is a benefit to them and their fellow students if they can incorporate their prior knowledge into their assignments.

In addition, just because someone can answer questions about how to develop a presentation doesn't mean that person can actually develop a presentation. It is an advantage for students to practice in situations like those in real life within a learning venue rather than waiting until they get to a job situation. Our institutions and workplaces benefit when graduates are already adept at working in teams, comfortable at producing and presenting ideas to others, and knowing where to find information and communicating it to diverse audiences.

The question to ask is, "What is it I am trying to teach the students?" If the answer is, "How to write," then you need to see examples of their writing to know if they are able to write correctly. Answering multiple-choice questions about the correct way to write is not the same as demonstrating the ability to write. And if students need to know how to identify appropriate settings on a machine, then they need to be shown the machine and asked to identify the appropriate settings for specific situations, not answer multiple-choice or true-or-false questions about the correct settings.

If you don't measure the task itself, you just measure students' recognition of the terms of the task. The two are not the same. In addition to being certain you are measuring the correct thing, the assessment becomes much more interesting to the students and provides the students with more motivation and also more confidence when they have performed well.

To see how important authentic assessments are, would you rather have someone cut your hair who has made 100 percent on ten fifty-question multiple-choice tests about cutting hair but no experience, or someone who has actually cut the hair of multiple individuals but taken no written tests? And who would you rather have come to your aid when a pipe has broken at your home and water is spewing everywhere: Someone who has passed every written test for the past year on plumbing with no experience, or someone who has ridden along and watched and helped out with a plumber for six months on house calls?

Perhaps you think, "Those are skills jobs, and we are educating people." If so, ask yourself, "Aren't we teaching them to be able to do something when they are deemed educated?" What is that thing we are helping them learn how to do? Sometimes one challenge is to make certain we've identified correctly all the things we want them to learn and be sure we are teaching to the correct learning outcomes. But I think sometimes we misidentify what the actual teaching goals are. We say we want them to learn to identify X number of muscles on a mammal in the lab, but what we really mean is we want them to learn to work in a team, develop cooperation skills, learn how it feels to cut on something, understand the texture of muscles, and be able to identify the difference in appearance of fat, muscles, and connective tissues. Those are very different outcomes and require a different sort of teaching than simply identifying muscles.

By assigning students a grade in a course, we are declaring that they have certain skills and knowledge. My question is, Have we accurately assessed those skills we intended to teach?

Quizzes

If you are going to use quizzes for assessment, and these are appropriate in some situations, it is important to have more than one version of the quiz. Using question alternates works well. I also found it was best to prepare a question for every competency and then write question alternates. Questions sets may be created for each competency with multiple question alternates for each competency, so each person may be given a different combination of questions for the test. I like to have at least three alternates for each question. I prefer five alternates, but I learned how time-consuming that is. I found that I'd write five alternates for the first five competencies. Then, when I realized time was running out, I'd have to scramble to create only one question for each of the final twenty competencies. Once again, learn from my mistakes so you don't have to suffer through them yourself.

Teaching for the Long Term

What if you knew your students were going to be tested six months following the completion of your course, and you would be held legally liable for any portion of the course the students did not remember? How would you teach differently? Would you:

- Reduce the amount of material you cover?

- Make sure you don't overload the students with extraneous information?

- Give the information in a format relative to their learning modes?

- Ask them for the most helpful format in order for them to learn?

- Care how they received the information as long as they learned it?

- Care if they were coming to class or staying home as long as they were learning the material and giving feedback that they were learning?

- Care about the "copyright" of your lectures if you were held liable for the future performance of our students?

How much attention would you pay to your presentation under these circumstances?

- Would you prepare in advance?

- Would you change the quiz questions?

- Would you change the way you spent time during class?

- What sort of handouts and other learning aids would you offer?

- What would you want to know about your students before you began teaching them?

  - That they know how to study?

  - That they know how they learn best and give them to tools to do this?

  - That they know the best study and learning methods for them?

- Would your convenience be a factor in your teaching, or would their learning would be at the center of your concern?

- Would you be concerned about corralling them into a large group so you have to lecture only one time?

In this situation, here is what you would probably want to do:

- Check individually with each student to make sure that each person is getting the concepts.
- Make sure that each individual student understands the concepts on a comprehension and application level.
- Know what each student's weaknesses are so that you could invoke measures to support and correct those weaknesses.
- Get frequent feedback from them about how the course was going.
- Find out how they are understanding the material and whether the course needs any changes in order for them to comprehend things better.
- Find out if they are learning and retaining the material as early as possible and not wait until very far into the semester to verify.
- Make certain they understand the material, apply it to as many different situations as possible, have as much practice as needed, and integrate it into their everyday world and existing knowledge.
- Refer to previous information in each subsequent module and relate each concept to each of the other concepts, making certain the students had the context for each concept, the big picture, and how this all fits together.

If we know those are the ways we would go about things if we had to make sure the students still knew the content six months later, why don't we just make those changes now? I think my content is important enough for them to remember it in six months, and undoubtedly you do too. In some cases, it is important for them to be able to know it all of their careers, so if that is the case, it seems imperative that we take decisive measures to ensure we are teaching in such a way that students will retain the information for the long term. If the information we are teaching is not important enough for them to remember six months from now, then perhaps we should reexamine our content and find some more lasting ideas on which to spend our time and theirs in the course.

When I taught sophomore-year human anatomy and physiology, I knew the only reason each of the students was taking that course was that it was a prerequisite for another course. The students were going to a variety of places after my class: some to professional schools, for example. I understood that my success was really measured by how well those students were prepared for the next course they were going to take. During that next course was when they would find out whether I had done them justice or cheated them out of their tuition money and their time investment during the course. So how well they did in my course was really not the issue; much bigger issues were at stake.

I realized that many of the students did not know how to study, so I began teaching them how. The first thing we did was to take a learning styles inventory to find out how we learned best. Then we began to use that information. Second, I began to show them how to organize their study materials. Third, I gave them all of my notes and slides so they could take notes from my lecture onto the Power-Point presentation. Fourth, I presented material in small sections of information and reminded them they could learn as they went about their everyday lives. I would present a list of material and remind them this is a list they could learn while waiting for a child to finish a piano lesson, for example. Fifth, I related the new information I was presenting to something with which they were already familiar. We used lots of food analogies; for example, in a nerve, a myelin sheath was the bread around a corn dog, and the axon was the hot dog part.

Some students once suggested it would be easier to learn the muscles of the cat if they had a video to study by. I asked if they wanted to make the video themselves so the next group of students would have the video to study. This gave them an opportunity for active learning and an opportunity to teach other students, which reinforced their own learning as well. This project in fact taught us many things. In addition to the technology issues, the students learned persistence and commitment. When they ran into roadblocks and wanted to quit, I did not allow them to back out of the project. We brainstormed, found possible options, and moved ahead with the project. In the end, the students added music to the demonstration and were extremely proud of their work. Each of the students wanted a copy of the video to show their families.

The next year I offered the video to that year's student, but they had heard about the previous students making a video and also wanted to create a video and do better than the previous year's students. So what the student had originally thought would be a study aid was not the actual aid; the process of producing the aid was the actual aid.

When we know that we are responsible for students' learning, we begin to take the long-term view. In that same course on anatomy and physiology, I had the students learn Latin and Greek prefixes, suffixes, and root words. Understanding the meaning of these terms would give them the ability to determine, at least partially, the meanings of new terms they encountered without knowing anything about the word. This was a skill that would give them an advantage as they progressed in whatever field they chose. All semester, we had weekly quizzes about these terms. In the second semester, we repeated the groups of terms again so they would be revisiting those terms and reviewing and renewing their information. I encountered several students years later who told me was how helpful learning those Greek and Latin terms was and how it had given such an advantage over the other students in their courses in professional school.

Another thing we tend to do if we see ourselves on the same team with our students is to give them some of those hints and techniques we've learned over the years to help us recall information. Many of us have insider's secrets to ways to learn and remember, and as faculty members, sometimes we feel obligated to keep those to ourselves so the students will "think we're smart." In fact, they already know you're smart, and there is no need to keep a facade up in front of them that you are the all-knowing being.

Dissemination of information is no longer limited to faculty members. All of the course work from Massachusetts Institute of Technology, for example, is available on the Internet, and most other information is freely available as well. You are not the only source of information. Your value added now is very different from being the keeper of the information. You become the one who understands what is most important, and what the best way is to go about processes, and the one who is needed to communicate and allow the students to understand the concepts behind the facts. You are more than a dispenser of the facts.

In this situation, your goal is to establish a rapport with your students and a situation in which you want them to know you are on their team to help them get to the goal. You are not the person standing between them and the goal to try to keep them from the goal if they don't do well. Rather than the gatekeeper, we are all now their encouragers.

Questions for First Time Web-Based Instructors

I typically get the same several questions each time a new instructor begins teaching online. I'll answer those for you here.

How Do You Know It Is the Student Doing the Work?

One thing you can do is to have students turn in intermediate steps to the assignments so that you can learn the character and quality of their writing and work. For example, if students have to write a term paper, you might require that they turn in the following items at progressive dates along the way to the final paper:

- Topic
- Resources to use
- Draft outline
- Revised outline
- Two to three draft paragraphs and additional subpoints for other elements of outline
- Three to six draft paragraphs and additional subpoints for the remainder of outline
- Bibliography
- A rough draft of the paper
- The final rewritten paper, including the bibliography

With all of these steps, enough work is required that the student will have to show you work along the way. You can do the same thing for a speech or oral presentation or a lab project by asking to see all the intermediate steps. This also allows you to give feedback to the students (Chickering and Gamson, 1987). It helps them understand the development process for a major project, assists them with pacing themselves, and typically allows them to end up with a much better product in the end than if they had not had to turn in these intermediate products for review.

How Do You Know It Is the Student Taking The Test?

Unless you have the students use a Webcam (and you watch each one individually), you really do not know that the correct student is taking the text. In fact, the same situation exists in classes with large numbers of students: you do not know that the correct students are taking the test unless you check identification cards as they enter the classroom. Another option some faculty select is to have the students go to a testing center for their exams, where they must present their student identification. However, relying totally on exams for grades is not a recommended practice. Project-based assignments and other authentic assessments are more valuable.

How Do You Know They Aren't Looking at Their Books During the Test?

Unless you have them in a monitored environment, you don't. You just assume that they are looking at the books. Therefore, ask questions about concepts and the ideas, not sentences from the book.

In a freshman biology course, I actually told my students to have all their books, notes, study guide, and everything else they'd done for class all filled out right in front of them for the test. This policy encouraged them to do the exercises I'd assigned. It did not punish those few honest individuals who if I had said "no books" would have had "no books" and every else in the class would have had their books in front of them and thought nothing of it. Except to clarify spelling or some small point, the books and other study aids were of no help whatsoever (and I had told them this in advance). I was testing concepts and ideas, and asking them to apply these concepts and ideas. I was not lifting sentences out of the book and making multiple-choice questions out of them.

You are trading one commodity for another with the students. The commodity you have to trade is points; the commodity the students have to trade is time and effort. Therefore, if an assignment takes a large percentage of time and effort, it should be rewarded with a large number of points in your course. Conversely, if an assignment or test is a small effort and takes little time, it should have a small number of points in your course. If you want students to spend a lot of time on an assignment, you signal that by the number of points you attach to it.

Action Steps

Step 13

Here is a way to take a fresh look at your course. If it were up to you for your favorite niece or nephew to learn the first outcome, what would be the best way that person could learn that lesson? Are there some experiences she or he would need to have? Are there some books that would be useful? Are there some people you'd like him or her to meet? Set your timer for seven minutes, and using Form 7, Learning Process, write down all the ideas that come to mind

Time estimate: 7 minutes

Step 14

Repeat step 13 for each of the major points or outcomes for your course. You may not have time to do all of them right now, and that's fine; perhaps you'll have seven minutes again later today, maybe between two classes, or a couple of seven-minute time slots during lunch. Take the opportunity whenever it presents itself. If you have a copy of Form 7 handy, you'll get them finished in no time. Save the completed forms because you will work with them in Chapter Five.

Time estimate: Calculate by multiplying 7 minutes times the number of outcomes in your course

Step 15

Now assume that all of the information you have put down on Form 7 can be translated into the Web-based environment. The issue now is how to go about this. Here are some possibilities:

- If there are people to see, you can have a guest speaker in the course for a live chat, a conference call, or other types of synchronous sessions. (Refer to Finkelstein, 2006, for information on synchronous teaching.) If some students cannot attend, you might choose to archive a transcript of that session for them to view later.

- If experience is the best teacher for an outcome, consider opportunities in local communities for the students to visit the appropriate venues for these experiences. In a course on geriatrics and nutrition, one of our assignments for nursing students is to visit a local nursing home and sit near the feeding table so they can view the trays of individuals who need assistance eating. The students' task was to identify barriers to the patients' gaining weight. Trying to identify barriers without that experience would have been difficult.

- Provide links to appropriate readings.

- If there are relevant, and reputable, Web sites, ask students to find particular information from them. If you are using those sites as a reference yourself, it would be helpful for the students to seek out the information you went there to find. Often we remember things we look up better than things we were just told, so have them help hunt it down.

- Do you want them to be able to take a stance and defend their viewpoint? Create discussion questions that will foster this sort of dialogue.

These approaches will be much more interesting than the lecture method for both you and your students.

Use Form 7 to record the information.

Time estimate: Calculate by multiplying 7 minutes times the number of outcomes or major points in the course.

Step 16

Plan assessments for learning outcomes for each module. Use Form 7. Remember you are trying to determine the best way for a person to show you that they understand the concepts and competencies for your course. What evidence do you need to gather in order to verify the students have command of the content?

Time estimate: 20 to 40 minutes per module

Step 17

Develop appropriate assessment documents for the learning outcomes for each module.

Time estimate: 1 to 3 hours per module

Design with Organization in Mind

Introduction to learning guides

Upon completion of this chapter, the faculty member will:

- Recall two audiences for learning guides.
- Recall the purposes of learning guides.
- Recognize the elements of learning guides.
- Gather references for learning modules.
- Develop learning guides for all modules.
- Create course development map.
- Prioritize portions of course to place online first.

Learning Resources

Required resources

- Chapter 4 *Conquering the Content*

Learning Activities

Activities for this lesson

- Document objectives or learning outcomes for each module using Form 9 in Appendix A.
- Document content, required resources, activities, and assessments for each module using Form 9 in Appendix A.
- Prioritize most important elements of course to place online first, using information on Form 9 in Appendix A.

Self-Assessment	
Check your understanding	• Ability to develop workable learning guides

Lesson Evaluation	
"Graded" assessments or evidence to proceed	• Learning guides will be used to guide development of Web-based course.

A learning guide is a succinct checklist that contains everything students need to do for one module. It also serves as a succinct planning and development guide for the faculty member in planning the course. Subsequently it provides a checklist to use for course development.

Learning guides will serve as the blueprint from which to develop a course; therefore, anything you need to create or place in the learning management system for a module will be placed on the learning guide. This is where references to textbook pages and chapter numbers appear. In fact, this is the only place where there are references to specifics of the textbook. Remember that you are trying to ensure that your course is easily updatable. When textbook references appear only on this page in the course materials, you know exactly where to go to alter chapter and page references when the textbook changes. You will never add items to the calendar, syllabus, assignments, or anywhere else online without updating this page.

After you have developed learning guides for each module, you will look at the entire course and set priorities before developing the individual components of the guide. The prioritization process will be based on the amount of time you have before the course begins and on the most irritating or time-consuming aspects of your course, which you identified on Form 3 (Course Revision Thoughts).

With the student's perspective in mind, we will be providing a checklist, or "to-do" list, for them to complete. Everything students need to access or complete for a module will appear on the learning guide for that module. In other words, if it is an expectation for the students, it needs to be on the learning guide.

Learning Guide Development

This chapter and Chapter Five are the most challenging in the book. If you do not complete the exercises in this chapter, developing your course will be more difficult for you to accomplish.

Planning your course through these learning guides is the key to good course organization, which in turn is the key to your students' being confident of their direction in the course. It is also your ticket to a semester that is not filled with telephone calls, e-mails, and questions regarding process in the course. In other words, the payoff for the exercises in this chapter is big. The format set out here has worked for me and for many of my colleagues. If this format does not work for you, then alter it or make up one of your own, but some type of organizer like this for your students and your own planning will prove to be very helpful.

Elements of the Learning Guide

The following items are found in a learning guide. These form the essential elements to outline information students will be learning.

Module and Course Identification

Learning Outcomes

Learning Resources

Learning Activities

Self-Assessment

Lesson Evaluation

Identification

Make certain that the learning guide is identified with the course title and module name. It may be that other courses have also adopted learning guides, and students should be able to distinguish the guide for your course and module at a glance. It might be helpful to have a tiny visual of the course outline to the side with this topic highlighted within the outline you provided at the beginning of the course.

Learning Goals or Outcomes, or "What You Need to Know"

I found that first- and second-year undergraduate students are more comfortable with casual titles. Use the ones I have here, or create a variation of your own that is customized for your students.

Spend some time to make the learning outcomes or objectives meaningful. You can often find a version of these in your instructor's manual, but is that really what you teach? Use those published objectives as a basis to customize the learning outcomes for the course you teach. Few faculty members follow an entire textbook; the objectives will also probably need to be altered. Some institutions have distinct preferences about using "objectives" or "learning outcomes" or other names. Alter the title and formatting to suit your situation.

Learning Resources, or "Tools to Help You Learn"

These are the references students will need to access for this module. It is helpful to divide these into "required resources" and "additional resources" categories.

List any presentation of content here. Perhaps you have supplied course notes, online text, some type of video or audio, or a slide presentation in your Web-based course. Note these in the content section, and provide the link to those resources so students will know where to find them. References to textbook pages go here. This is the *only* place in the course to list textbook pages and chapter references.

Links to journal articles, Web sites, or other resources students will use for this module belong here too. If you list a Web site or link, you also need to provide additional information for students:

- What do you want the students to do with that link? Is that a major task or a minor one?

- Do you want them to just skim the contents or grasp the details?

- Is this an overview or a detailed version of an important concept?

Give students the context into which this Web site falls and the reason they are directed to it:

- What are they supposed to do when they get there?

- What are the supposed to bring back?

- Where do they turn this in?

If you can't answer those questions, reconsider whether the link should be included.

Distinguish between required references and supplemental ones. Supplemental references are helpful for students who want to explore the topic further, but make it clear that those are optional references for students who want to complete the assignment and quickly move forward.

Learning Activities, or "What You Need to Do"

List specific assignments here. Perhaps you have discussion questions for the students to answer or an assignment for them to complete. Remember that this is a checklist they are using to make sure they do all their work, so anything that needs to be completed should be listed.

For each assignment, students need this information:

- What to do.
- How to do it.
- How it will be graded, that is, what is important and what is not important in grading.
- How many points it is worth.
- How these points compare to the overall number of points in the course.
- How this falls into the context of the course. Is this a large, major assignment or topic or a lesser or minor point?
- Where they turn in the assignment.
- What they call this assignment. (Provide the file names.)
- How they should label this assignment.
- What to type in the subject line.
- How they turn it in.
- The time it is due.
- What sorts of reference materials they should use to complete this assignment.
- Whether collaboration with other students is an option.

This looks like a daunting list, but answering these questions in advance will allow you and your students to avoid much confusion; moreover, the students will feel comfortable and confident that all is under control. It will also prevent you from having to answer these questions individually from the students. Once again, this up-front investment of time will pay off well later. It is easier than you think to get all these answers into your assignments.

Here is an assignment example that answers these questions:

- Cell Organelle: Individual project using current references provided in Module 01.
- Describe the function major of one organelle of a eukaryotic cell in 75–100 words.
- 50 points. [Link to grading rubric.] See sample assignment.
- Due October 21 at 5:00 P.M.
- Submit in the Assignments tool labeled: "Assignment 1."
- Label: "LastnameFirstnameA01."

Chickering and Gamson tell us to set high expectations, and part of setting expectations is modeling examples for students. Giving a sample completed assignment that you deem is excellent work is sometimes an appropriate option. In creative assignments, you might want to give students freedom to use their own imaginations and not limit their ideas to an example you provide. But on assignments in which you know what you want, it is good to show the students what that is. The more they understand your expectations, the more likely they are to meet them.

In order for students to understand how the assignment of points fits into the context of the entire course, it is helpful to have this worked out in advance. One easy way to figure points is to have all courses worth 1,000 points. You can plan this from the beginning. If you want the lab portion to be worth 30 percent, you can make it worth 300 points. Then you can adjust test scores accordingly. In this way, students will be clear about what their grades are at all times. Grades can be based on total points. It takes 900 points to get an A, 800 to get a B, and so forth.

Self-Assessment, or "How to Know If You're Ready for Grading"

Accrediting agencies suggest giving students an opportunity to assess their own learning progress before they are given a graded assessment. This is an opportunity for the students to find the weak areas in their knowledge and review them prior to the graded assessment.

Self-assessments are varied in format:

- Behavioral/clinical based: "You should be able to take blood pressure accurately within 2 minutes at least 3 times out of 4 attempts."
- A quiz: "You should be able to make a 100 percent on the practice quiz."
- A description of knowledge: "You should be able to define all the new terms in this chapter and be able to apply those terms in appropriate situations."
- Something in the textbook: "You should be able to complete all the review exercises at the end of the chapter."

Lesson Evaluation, or "How to Show Me What You've Learned"

Any opportunities the students will have for gaining points from this module should be listed here. It might be a quiz or an assignment on this module, or it may be the portion of the unit test that covers the module. Students need to know how and when they will be graded on this material.

Being familiar with the elements of a learning guide will allow you to make more informed decisions about how to divide your course into lessons.

Prioritizing in Creating Your Course

Once you have complete learning guides for each module of your course, take a realistic look at the amount of time you have between now and the beginning of the semester in which you will teach. It may be that there is no time, and your goal is simply to stay one or two weeks ahead of your students. I refer to this as the suicide method of course development. Both you and the students will have a very difficult semester. If it is all possible, perhaps you can take a blended approach so that you meet during some class periods and have supplemental materials online.

It is essential to set some priorities for the process of creating your Web-based course in case time runs out before the semester begins. Here I offer a few suggestions about some ways to prioritize the portions of your course on which to focus initially.

I advise that you answer two questions as you begin the process of prioritizing. The first question is, "What irritates me the most about my classroom course?" There are many possible answers—for example, "Students asking for another copy of the syllabus," "Students asking for test results," "Students asking for their grade average," or "Students asking for last week's notes."

Once you've determined your answer to the first question, you have identified a priority item to place online first. The most irritating thing to me was students asking me if I had the tests graded, followed by, "What's my grade average now?" As a result, I decided to put the exams online first. Students could see their results immediately following submission of the test, and they were also allowed to see their course average at any time. With the grades online, a student could check his or her grade repeatedly and never ask me about it a single time. The students were happy because they were able to look at their grades to their hearts' content, and I was happy because I didn't have to answer questions about grades.

The second question is, "What is the most time-consuming aspect of the course for me?" It may be any number of things: grading exams, posting grades, grading discussions, administering exams, giving out handouts, or giving quizzes. Your answer is another priority item to place online.

Often there are efficient ways of dealing with each of these issues in a Web-based course. Therefore, what might be extremely time-consuming if done manually may become a much faster process if automated electronically.

If you put the most irritating and the most time-consuming aspects of your current course into your Web-based course first, you will have an immediate pay-off: a positive outcome for this experience and a return on your time investment. With this additional time, you can work on other aspects of your Web-based course.

It is also very important, if you are skeptical about the entire concept of Web-based courses in general (and it is okay to be skeptical), to begin with something that gives you a positive payoff so that you are not investing time in a less rewarding portion of the course at the start. In the end, if it is up to you about which portions of your course to have online and which portions to retain for the classroom, you will have placed those most helpful to you online and left the other tasks for the classroom time.

Ideally we would place those knowledge transference portions of the course online and use the classroom time for integrative learning. The opportunity for students to interact with you and with each other to incorporate the content they are learning with discussion and application is very beneficial to their learning. Opportunities to learn from you how to use the concepts will elevate the value of your expertise and therefore their time with you. Draves (2002) suggests that cognitive learning is more efficient online than in the classroom and that integrative learning is more effective in the classroom when that cognitive learning has taken place online, leaving more time for the communication to take place in the classroom.

The Rewards of Preparation Time

It is critical that you know what is going to happen throughout your course before the semester begins. The suicide method of course development (trying to stay one to two weeks ahead of the students) is troublesome for everyone in the course and everyone around you.

All design and development activities should be completed before the semester begins. And any preparation time you spend prior to the semester will save you time during the semester. In my experience, if I waited until during the semester to do those same tasks, it took me ten to thirty times as long as if I had addressed those tasks before the semester began. The time investments in course design and development prior to the beginning of the course are wise ones.

How to Set Priorities

If you plan to make six videos for each of the twenty major points of content you've developed and there are only ten weeks between now and the beginning of the semester, you may (wisely) determine that those 120 videos are not going to happen this semester. So it is important for you to find the three most difficult concepts and make videos on only those concepts in the coming weeks. Or if you've planned to develop one case study with a complex story line that ties in concepts from each of the twenty chunks you've developed, you may determine that twenty individual case vignettes would be simpler for you to write.

At the base of the priority triangle in Figure 4.1 is the largest segment of the triangle; it represents the items that must be done for your course. The next

Figure 4.1: Priority Triangle

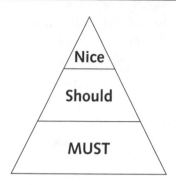

largest segment represents items that should be done for your course, and the top segment represents those items that it would be nice to do for your course. I consider the learning guides a must item. Prior to making your home page look nice or anything else in your course, the content needs to be in order. Whether the course is appealing is secondary to the need for the learning principles to be in place. The first impression will matter, but after that, students want to log in, get to the course materials, get their work finished, and move on to another part of their life. Most are not looking to you for their artistic enlightenment for the week.

It is important to map out your entire course based on this priority triangle. (I learned this the hard way, so trust me on this.) Do the must things for the entire course; then come back and add another layer to the course if there is more time; then move to what would be nice to have. Otherwise you will end up with an award-winning module 1 and nothing for any other models because you've used up all the time you had to do this. At the last minute, you'll end up loading straight text documents, and the students will be incredibly disappointed after that striking and rich module 1.

In my experience, it works best if you do must things for the entire course and then come back and add layers of elements to your course so that the entire course looks uniform. Also, it is best not to spend an inordinate amount of time on the colors of the home page, your PowerPoint slides, and other online material. Most programs have templates designed by graphic artists with training in color coordination. Typically we instructors can't do a lot better than they have. We will be more effective pouring our creativity and energy into our teaching rather than into color alterations. In addition, the background images on PowerPoint are extremely large, and unless you have a compression program like Impatica, providing a presentation without any background helps access times.

Resource Gathering

After developing your learning guides, take them with you to the library or visit your library's electronic resources to access the articles you need for your course. You will be able to do this efficiently since you have listed all the articles you need. You can look up the links to all the journal articles to make certain students have library access to link to them. My hope is that your library has subscriptions to online journals and you have the ability to link directly from your course to the journal. If so, this direct linking is typically considered the best approach.

You might talk with your librarian about copyright requests for these articles and recommendations about the best way to gain access to them for your students. Some facilities have access to a Citrix server, where articles and images sensitive to copyright may be stored so students can have access without compromising the integrity of the materials. Other provisions may be in place at your institution.

Every institution has different ways of working with academic computing, library staff, Web-based learning staff, and information technology staff who are involved in these types of resources. You should get to know all of these individuals because you depend on them for your courses, and you want them to know you and know you are cooperative and congenial. You might survive a few weeks if the boss is mad at you, but if the person who helps you get over the bumps in your Web-based course is mad at you, life can be unbearable.

Let's say you need twenty quizzes, so when you have five to ten minutes between meetings or are waiting for someone, you can churn out a quiz question or two. Or maybe you want students to do an assignment four times during the semester and want to create a form for it. If you are among the fortunate who have assistance with course development, you can be much more organized by saying, "I need these twenty quizzes, and these are the questions," rather than coming to that person twenty different times and saying, "Here's another quiz."

Web-Based Aspects of the Course

Equipment

Have you ever had to make a presentation when the equipment was different from what you had been told or you attended a presentation where the equipment didn't match what the presenter had brought? Maybe the presenter brought materials for a computer and an LCD project, but the meeting site was prepared for someone with transparencies. Unless there is a way of transferring information quickly from one format to another or a way to improvise on the fly, the entire exchange of information may be compromised. The same is true if you do not plan your Web-based course as a Web-based course from the beginning. If you've been teaching a classroom course for years and show up to a Web-based course with your classroom materials, it's like standing in front of a computer and an LCD projector trying to figure out a place from which to transmit your transparencies. There is no such place. Those two modes of communication are not compatible.

In *Learner-Centered Teaching* (2002), Maryellen Weimer points out that "the piecemeal addition of new techniques does not transform teaching." Instead we need to approach change systematically. "Systematic change means change that is planned, prepared, and then implemented according to some process"(p. 185). The course must be planned as a Web-based course from the start. That is why we began with revisiting the goals and learning outcomes in Chapter One and brainstorming the best way to teach those outcomes. With Web-based technology, there are some limitations and freedoms not offered to us when teaching by other delivery modes.

Technology

Gratuitous use of technology is not impressive to students. They've seen much better than what we are able to place into a learning management system, so using a tool just to use it is not helpful. There should be an educational reason for use of the tools in your course. The course content is to be the challenge of the course, not the use of the technology. If there are tools your students may be unfamiliar with, providing instructions for how to use them is vital.

During one semester, a faculty member I was working with had learned to use the Assignments tool in WebCT, and she was interested in having the students use that to turn in their final paper. We talked about the way the students had turned in their other papers throughout the semester, which was as an attachment in the system e-mail. But no other papers were due prior to the major final paper. My suggestion was that the students' stress level was going to be rather high for getting their final paper completed anyway, and introducing a new tool to go along with the assignments itself would be additional stress. She agreed and waited until the next semester to use the Assignments tool. In that situation, the technology was not going to be an enhancement, and it was not going to be invisible. Her conclusion was that although it would be much more efficient for her, it was better for the students not to introduce a new tool at that point in the semester.

Choosing the Most Important Topics

Let's say that your students are going to remember only five to nine major competencies from one lecture. What competencies would you want them to be? You would have to choose them very wisely, perhaps remembering this point: "It is better to understand new material than simply to memorize it by rote. If new material is well understood, then a few forgotten details can be derived from the context of what has been remembered. In contrast, if rote-memorized material is forgotten, it is gone" (Steen, 2007, p. 135).

Let's say that you've chosen those competencies. You'll begin by focusing on one of them. This is a segment of learning, and within this, you can also get across five to nine points. We will call each of these items a *chunk*. Which five to nine chunks would you like for them to remember? Would it be better to present a hundred things and take potluck on what they remember? Or would it be better for you, the subject matter expert, to select the most important chunks so that there is complete understanding about those points, you have a record of what students who leave your course know, and you can build on those concepts?

Accepting reality is the biggest challenge here. After this, the issues are much easier to deal with. If you continue to operate under the assumption that the students are remembering every word you say (in reality, they never do), then you will continue to fight against reality for the remainder of the semester. If you align yourself with reality from the beginning and even relax into that, then the remainder of the semester will be much easier. If reality is that students remember only about five concepts I present, then as the subject matter expert, I want to determine those five concepts. Then we can move to the next competency and select the next five important concepts. Rather than fighting reality all semester,

I now am working with reality and using it to my advantage. Therefore, life gets easier.

What you choose to believe does not alter the truth. The truth is that students will not remember all of the content. Other truths are that your course usually is not the only one the students are taking and that school is most likely not the most important part of their life. I know this seems limiting, and you no doubt are thinking, "There is no way that I can cut back on my material that much." But remember that dealing with reality is better than continuing to fight it.

Think about this. If you cover the maximum that the research is supporting a student can absorb at one time, that is nine items. If you cover seven competencies in one module and present five to nine concepts about each of those competencies, your students actually understand each one. This means that they have just learned up to sixty-three concepts on one module. I think that is great! And what we are going to do is focus on those most meaningful elements of the course and develop learning around the chunks.

Instructional Guidance

Instructional guidance plays an important role in learning from visual representations, particularly when instruction requires active construction of knowledge. Sometimes the free exploration of multimedia presentations can impose a heavy cognitive load (Cook, 2006).

Often multimedia materials are available that are far superior to anything we have the time or the expertise to create. I encourage you to use those whenever possible so you are not spending your development time on something that already exists. It would be better to address places where there are gaps or holes in the existing material. However, when you send students to the Web site of a publisher or another Web site where a video or animation is available, provide a framework and some guidance for them to this learning experience. For example, the students will benefit from an explanation of what they will be viewing, the key points to watch for, and if there are specific segments of great significance. You might say something like, "Watch for the yellow circle representing the neurotransmitter to be released from the dendrite [nerve ending]."

Action Steps

Step 18

Create the learning objectives or outcomes (based on the competencies from Form 6) for each module. Use Form 9 for this purpose.

Time estimate: 1–4 hours

Step 19

Complete the learning guide for each module in the course. This will mean completing the remainder of Form 9 for this purpose.

Time estimate: 15–35 hours

Design with
Content in Mind

Learning Activities	
Activities for this lesson	• Chunk course content into absorbable pieces of information. • Create bridges.

Self-Assessment	
Check your understanding	• Divide major points of course competencies into five- to nine-minute segments. • Be able to create bridges between content chunks.

Lesson Evaluation	
"Graded" assessments or evidence to proceed	• Create content chunks for course materials in each module. • Create introductions, reviews, and transitions for chunks in each module.

In Chapter One I noted that online learning is different from classroom learning because of the environment. In a Web-based environment, students are no longer surrounded by a room full of other students who are all focused on the same subject for fifty minutes of protected time. Instead, interruptions become part of the expectations of Web-based learning, and they require your course content to have these components:

Short, directed learning segments, or chunkability. Chunking is grouping pieces of information into meaningful segments. If your content is chunked, it is divided into short segments of passive learning, followed by an opportunity for active learning on those same concepts to reinforce the principle just introduced.

Ability to repeat and review content, or repeatability. Students need the option to replay segments of presentations to review content. Repetition of content helps move information from short-term memory into long-term memory (Clark, Nguyen, and Sweller, 2006). It is important to be able to replay a small portion of a presentation for clarification purposes without having to listen to the entire presentation.

Ability to stop and resume without having to start all over, or pauseability. Some interruptions can be taken care of quickly, and the student is back to the presentation almost right away, but those few seconds of a presentation may have been crucial. It is better for the student to be able to pause and hear everything you are saying than to have to start from the beginning in order to get just a few words. Chances are that student will not have time to come back to that presentation again just for a few words. Adding a pause option increases the likelihood that students will absorb all of the content.

Clear, direct, instructions, or understandability. Instructions in the Web-based environment have to be extremely clear. Things can be misinterpreted or misunderstood, or the tone perceived differently than you intended. You've probably experienced this through miscommunications with written e-mails. It is very important for your own time management issues that the instructions in your course are easy to follow. Then you won't be answering logistical questions during the semester rather than spending your time interacting with the students about the content. Your learning guides will assist you in developing clear, direct instructions.

In order for your content to have these components, you will have to modify the content of your existing course materials. First, you will have to focus on the content. In the classroom, generally the main focus is on the teacher, but in a Web-based learning course, the main focus is on the content. This is another reason the content requires modification. Now the content will be designed to include directives about how to proceed, when to move to specific activities, when to interact with other students, and so forth. Whereas in the classroom you could have directed these activities on the fly, those now all have to be planned out in advance and incorporated into the content.

Second, in a Web-based environment, you have to focus on interactions by being more purposeful about creating situations for interaction among the students. Giving a topic and the instruction to discuss it is insufficient in a threaded discussion. In an asynchronous (not all at the same time) situation, it is important to give some specifics about what to discuss. For example, at the beginning of the semester, if you tell the students in the classroom, "Tell us about yourself," that means something different to each student. Some are reluctant to speak to the entire class and even tell their name, while others would ramble on for a half-hour if given the opportunity. So we generally say something like, "Tell us your name, where you are from, your major, and what you had for breakfast this morning [or some other nonthreatening fact]." So it is online when it comes to discussion questions. It is important to give the students something to discuss—for example,

"Choose to either support or oppose continued teaching of cursive writing, and give two reasons for your chosen stance."

Introduction to Chunking

George Miller, a Harvard University psychologist, experimented in 1956 to find the capacity of human working memory. He found that when given a list of unrelated items, a typical adult can recall between five and nine of them. Forty years later, Garrison, Anderson, and Archer (2001) found that "chunking the content into absorbable pieces helped keep students from feeling overwhelmed and provided them with the essential information for completing the exercises and grasping the concepts without exhausting them with too much written content" (p. 7). This also relates to creating schemata or scaffolding from which to recall information, which we address later. First let's compare information that is not chunked to that which is.

A Chunking Demonstration

On the next page is an image (Figure 5.1). View this image for three seconds. Then cover it with a plain piece of paper, and draw on another piece of paper what you remember seeing.

Figure 5.1

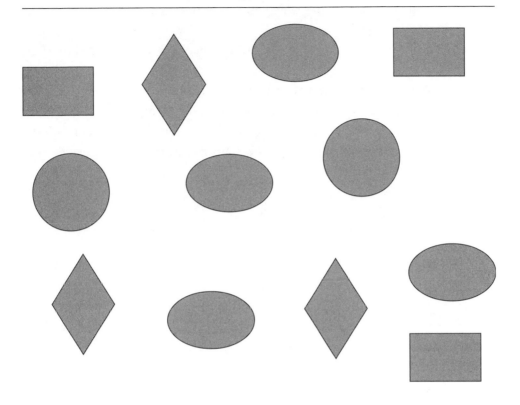

Look at Figure 5.2 for three seconds, cover it with a plain piece of paper, and draw on another piece of paper what you remember seeing. I bet you do better with the second image.

Look back at the two images. The only difference was the arrangement of the items.

You weren't viewing different content in these two images, only different arrangements of content. So when we chunk, we aren't asking the students to learn anything less; we are only grouping the content into meaningful segments. We still expect them to retain all the same information, but it has been placed into absorbable pieces of information.

Figure 5.2

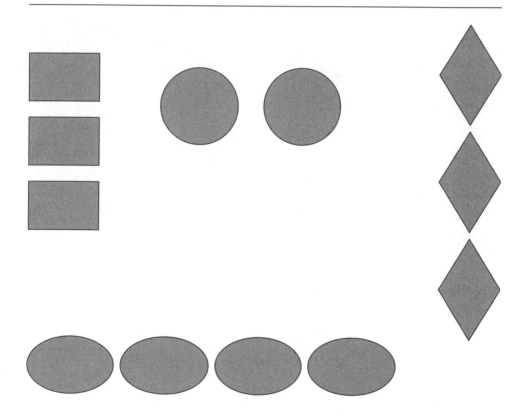

Let's try another example of chunking. Look at Figure 5.3 for three seconds, cover it with a piece of paper, and draw what you remember on another piece of paper. Was it easier to remember than Figure 5.1 because the images were chunked?

Figure 5.3

The information you are presenting to students is typically totally new to them. They are often learning new vocabulary, new concepts, and new hierarchical arrangements of the information all at the same time in your course, and it can be difficult for them to make sense of any of the information.

Let's look again at Figure 5.3. Are the two types of arrows more closely related (Figure 5.4), or are the blunt-ended half-circles more closely related to the half-circles with arrows (Figure 5.5)? Are the balloons all grouped together (Figure 5.6), or should all the things with points be grouped together (Figure 5.7) and all the objects with blunt ends all grouped together (Figure 5.8)? If they are organized by blunt versus pointed, the two objects in Figure 5.9 fit both categories, so what do you do with them?

Figure 5.4

Figure 5.5

Figure 5.6

Figure 5.7

Figure 5.8

Figure 5.9

These questions will be in the students' minds because they don't know the content like you do. They don't even know what names to call these objects (neither do I). There is much information to be communicated in the original slide.

Although the information has been chunked, there is still a lot of processing that needs to happen with that original presentation of the image. A single slide may turn out to take several minutes of explanation and further time for reflection by the students. Even though your presentation may be five to nine minutes long, by the time the students have digested and processed that information, it will typically take anywhere from two to four times as long for them to grasp or process the content. So a five-minute presentation can turn into a ten- or twenty-minute presentation for the students by the time they take notes and comprehend what you are presenting. The length of viewing the presentation will fall back to the original five minutes after they learn the concepts and are using the presentation simply for review.

Benefits of Chunking

Chunking has these benefits:

- Increased retention and understanding result.
- Accessing course materials will be more convenient.
- Students may cover more material.
- Results are measurable.
- Comprehension may be greater.

Miller's rule about adults being able to remember seven plus or minus two items affects adult learning. Content presented in one long segment is much less effective for learning than the same content broken down into several smaller segments. Pomales and Liu (2006) found that as module length increased from seven minutes to fourteen and then to twenty-one, students were less likely to complete the modules.

Presenting your course content as chunks offers students a number of advantages:

- If students know they can get something done in twenty minutes, they are more likely to log in when they have a break and less likely to postpone logging in until they have a large block of time.

- A student who logs in to the course more frequently is more likely to keep up.
- If your instructions are clear, concise, and easy to find, your course will be more pleasant for students to deal with and therefore less likely to put it off.
- You will be able to update your course easily.
- You will be able to add content to your course in small segments.
- You will be able to add to your course in modular components, which makes for a less daunting update task.
- If your course is chunked and a student's other courses aren't and the student had thirty minutes to study, whose course do you think the student will log into?

For students who prefer to view longer segments, all the material is there, and they can work on one segment after the other without a break. Presenting content in this manner provides options for students with a variety of needs. They are able to self-select the amount of content they are prepared to take in at one sitting.

Steps to Chunking

I've been guiding you to this point of how to accomplish chunking throughout this book, but I just haven't brought it to your attention until now. I am assuming you have already completed Forms 6 and 7 (if you haven't, do so before continuing), so chunking the content will be simple. The process I set out here will work regardless of the subject matter you are teaching.

I began teaching this way in the classroom when I wanted my students to work their studying into their everyday lives. I would present the information in small bits and encourage them to review it while they were in line somewhere, or waiting for an appointment, or other times when they had a few spare minutes. It proved to be very successful for them.

The Chunking Process

Chickering and Gamson (1987) document that time on task and interaction with the content are important ways to facilitate learning, so it is our job to assist students through the content. Our challenge is to guide them through the content but still create active learning opportunities for them. In order to accommodate memory processing, it is best to present five to nine minutes of passive learning followed by an opportunity to reinforce that concept with a participatory learning activity. We can do this in any number of ways.

First, it will be helpful to identify the learning segments by documenting the concept and the reinforcement activity that will help seal this content in the minds of the students and then place the introduction and transition statements between the chunks. On Form 8, you listed the major points you plan to cover in this topic. Now use Form 10 to surround each of those concepts with an introduction and reinforcement plus a transition to the next concept. This gives each concept some context so it is not an isolated idea; students gain some understanding of how all of the concepts are interrelated to each other. You will need one copy of Form 10 for each of your major points.

Before you move on to producing the chunks themselves, it is important to understand how the brain processes information.

How the Brain Processes Information

Cognitive Load

Cognitive load theory is a universal set of learning principles that are proven to result in efficient instructional environments as a consequence of leveraging human cognitive learning processes (Clark, Nguyen, and Sweller, 2006). Three main types of cognitive load have to be taken into consideration in order to minimize wasteful forms of cognitive load and maximize the useful forms (Clark, Nguyen, and Sweller, 2006):

- *Intrinsic load.* This is mental work imposed by the complexity of the content and determined by your instructional goals (Clark, Nguyen, Sweller, 2006). This makes a difference if portions of the tasks must be coordinated in the memory in order to happen and is thus more complex than a series of calculations or memory exercises (Clark, Nguyen, and Sweller, 2006).

- *Germane load.* This is mental work imposed by instructional activities that benefit the instructional goal (Clark, Nguyen, Sweller, and 2006).

- *Extraneous load.* This is mental work that is irrelevant to the learning goal and consequently wastes limited mental resources and drains mental capacity (Clark, Nguyen, and Sweller, 2006).

To create efficient instruction, we need to maximize germane load and minimize extraneous sources of load. Although you usually cannot control the intrinsic load associated with the learning goals, you can manage it by segmenting and sequencing content in ways that optimize the amount of element interactivity required at any one time (Clark, Nguyen, and Sweller, 2006)

Organization of Prior Learning

Experts have schema that enable the working memory to function much more efficiently. Clark, Nguyen, and Sweller (2006) call this process *automaticity;* it can allow us to largely bypass working memory limits. Novices do not have these schema and therefore need structures within the learning environment to substitute for them in processing information. For example, if I say, "Each of the mammals in North America is found in the Cincinnati Zoo," I am assuming some prior knowledge that may or may not be present in my students. In order to understand that statement, the student would have to know this information:

- What mammals are
- What countries are in North America
- Where Cincinnati is
- Whether Cincinnati is a county, state, or city
- What a zoo is

Anyone who knows this information will consider my sentence a very simple one, but anyone lacking this information will find this sentence and any other information on the topic difficult to understand.

Now I say, "The pronotal expansion in *Gargaphia* is typically more open than that of *Leptopharsa.*" Prior knowledge required here includes knowing this information:

- What a pronotal expansion is
- What *Gargaphia* is
- What "more open" means
- What *Leptopharsa* is

Then I proceed to tell you that this is because the cells in *Gargaphia* are generally larger in diameter than those of *Leptopharsa,* and the cell margins in *Gargaphia* are typically thinner than those of *Leptopharsa.* Are you continuing to follow my line of thinking? Most likely not, in particular if you hear this information and have no knowledge of how to spell *Gargaphia or Leptopharsa* and if I am giving you no visual images of either of these organisms (they are insects) or the parts of their anatomy to which I am referring. You can see how difficult it is for a novice to go along when information is not clear.

To promote understanding, I should have an image of *Gargaphia* and *Letopharsa,* be able to show where a pronotum is and what the pronotal expansion is, and be able to show a comparison of larger and smaller cells and thick and thin cell margins.

Information-processing theories assume that individuals have a limited working memory, and when it is overloaded, no learning will take place. Primarily it is the learner's prior knowledge that determines how much information can be held simultaneously in working memory. In general, the less prior knowledge a learner has, the more prone he or she is to cognitive overload (Cook, 2006).

Instructional Design Considerations

Dual-Mode Effect Visual and verbal information are processed in independent portions of the working memory, so these do not compete with each other. Therefore, presentations that take advantage of both the visual (graphics) and the verbal (text or audio) are more beneficial than those that use only one of them (Cook, 2006). This also explains why it is not useful to have a PowerPoint slide that you read to the students: both present verbal information that is processed in the same way, so you are not giving any additional information. A better approach would be to present a graphical representation of some phenomenon and then an audio narration over that graphic.

Split-Attention Effect When the design of the graphic does not foster the coordination of visual and verbal material, integration can be difficult because the learner's attention is split between the two modes of information. This process of integration imposes a heavy extraneous cognitive load for novice learners, especially when the material is highly detailed with a need to coordinate many labels with graphical information.

One way to reduce the cognitive load inducing search for a graphical element referenced in the verbal information is to present related material contiguously in space and time (Wu and Shah, 2004). When material is presented contiguously in time and space, learners are better able to form associations between the visual and verbal material (Chandler and Sweller, 1992). So placing the text explanation on the drawings or having a mouse-over explanation is helpful. Another way to reduce search time is to color-code related graphical and textual elements (Kalyuga, Chandler, and Sweller, 1999).

Modality Principle This principle holds that an audio explanation of visuals leads to better learning than a text explanation of visuals (Clark, Nguyen, and Sweller, 2006). This can be accomplished by adding narration to graphics or audio files to PowerPoint presentations.

Presentation Length An interesting study by Pomales-Garcia and Liu (2006) asked participants to watch content modules. They could complete the module, return later and finish a module, or quit and not complete the module. As module length increased from seven to twenty minutes, completion rates went down and pause and quit rates increased. These results suggest that quitting, pausing, or completing a Web module in one session has more to do with the length of the module than with the format (text, audio, or video) with which the module is delivered.

Presentation of Information Using the breaks between short segments as an opportunity to reinforce the concept just presented will allow the student to initiate the process of reassociating that information with previous knowledge, recalling the new information again, and giving the brain a chance to begin to make connections for storing that information into long-term memory. Sometimes I think of it sort of like brushing my teeth; one dainty swipe of the toothbrush is not going to remove all of those germs, particularly if I've eaten lots of sweets (crowded my brain with lots of competing information) or if it's been a long time since I've heard those concepts. The more brush strokes I can give at once, the better (up to a point). What is even better is if I brush my teeth twice a day. Brushing them more often will keep them cleaner than if I wait an entire week and brush them for twenty minutes all at once. They might look clean that one day, but three days later, they're not going to look clean no matter how long I brushed them three days ago.

Using Knowledge of Brain Processing

When you have a lot of information, you have to address that information frequently at small intervals so things will not begin to fall through the cracks. Therefore, dividing the learning into short segments followed by active learning reinforcement that may be covered in frequent sessions is more beneficial than long segments.

One of the most important things you can do is verbalize your thinking process to your students. Learning your reasoning process and how you process information in your discipline is very important. This is one of those things that must be learned from a mentor. Allowing your students to see these thinking paths is a major contribution you can make in developing students.

It is also important to have students verbalize their thinking back to you so you will have an opportunity to correct their reasoning processes as they form. Creating a safe environment for this process is one of the responsibilities for faculty members. Creating this safe place in a Web-based course may be accomplished by providing students with an opportunity to write in a journal, or you can develop a self-reflection component for your course. Having students think about their thinking reinforces the concepts being covered and thus builds in repetition of information, which is going to strengthen their learning.

Chunking for a Text-Based Lecture or Content Presentation

For text-based information, you will need to have some visuals to tell students where they are in the process, anchor the information with a scaffold of five to nine concepts, within each concept have five to nine key points, and within each key point, have a number of facts or major points. Make sure that students always know where you are in that scaffolding so that they are not lost. This can be easy to do with short pages that group together or are linked back to the beginning or are illustrated with a flowchart or have a tabbing structure to which the students may refer.

It is helpful to add any appropriate images to assist with absorbing and processing the content. Words and pictures are processed in different ways by the brain, and engaging both processes makes it more likely that the material will be remembered (Steen, 2007).

It is best not to have students scroll down the screens; a better choice is to have multiple pages that students click through. After a major concept is presented and illustrated, students need an opportunity to interact with that content in an active way in order to reinforce the concept in their mind.

It is important that we keep the focus on the concepts and cue the students in on which portions of the information we are giving them are concepts and which portions are there for context. Since students are unfamiliar with all of the information, it is easy for them to get hung up on support information and miss an idea that has major significance. This is one reason that parenthetical comments can be a danger. Although sidelights keep the course interesting and keep you from being bored, unless we give students an outline or a visual of the essential concepts, they cannot be certain when we are presenting a sidelight and when we are addressing crucial information. "A good teacher," writes Steen (2007), "can help students by refraining from pointless digressions; such digression may be interesting, but they also fill up short-term memory with unrelated facts. Information loss seems to occur when new data actually interferes with data that is already in working memory" (p. 135). Meaning tangential information may interrupt coding of the working memory. It is better to give the entire overview, drill down into some details, and then refer back to the overall structure of the information prior to drilling down into the next set of details.

After you complete Form 9, look at the material left over since you have extracted these major concepts from your lecture. Ask yourself what value is added by that left-over content. If your arch enemy on campus could justify to you there are pedagogical reasons to use this material in his or her course, then use it. If not, perhaps you need to question why you feel the reason for leaving it in.

Research indicates that presenting verbal information in spoken form rather than written form is more likely to increase the capacity of working memory, As for visual information, the use of static graphics rather than animations tends to be beneficial for enhancing learning except when representing motion or trajectory (Cook, 2006).

If you have a PowerPoint presentation you normally show in the classroom as you lecture, you can use portions of the same presentation to create the chunked course content. You just need to alter it a bit to be suitable for Web-based learning. Impatica presentation software is very helpful for delivering PowerPoint presentations. It compresses the file by about 90 percent so that the files students view are very small and there are no issues with download speeds. In addition, Impatica allows you to add narration to the presentation, so students will view the slides along with the narration (lecture) you would have normally presented in the classroom. You might also want to provide a pdf file of handouts for the PowerPoint presentation, which gives students a convenient place to take notes.

There are natural breaks in virtually all presentations. A transition in topics, change of focus, or difference in hierarchy levels are all cues that indicate natural breaks. In general, you can find these breaks every ten to twelve slides; we call these chunks. This is not a hard and fast rule, and segments vary in length. You may find your content naturally falls into a different pattern of lengths. Take one presentation, and find these breaks (electronically or on paper). These will serve as content for your chunks from Form 9.

Bridges

Bridges assist in transitioning from one chunk of content to the next. A bridge contains three elements: (1) a summary statement of the current chunk; (2) a transition statement connecting one chunk to the next; and (3) an introductory statement for the next chunk. In the past I've been asked to give specific examples of how bridges work between chunks of content. Here is an example:

Chunk 1

Bridge: We have now learned the seven steps for cleaning the outside of the car. Now that the outside of the car looks nice, notice how dirty the inside of the car appears. In the next segment, we will learn six steps for cleaning the inside of a car.

Summary statement: We have now learned the *seven steps for cleaning the outside of the car.*

Transition statement: Now that the *outside of the car* looks nice, notice how dirty the *inside of the car* appears.

Introduction to next topic: Next we will learn *six steps for cleaning the inside of a car.*

Bridge: After accomplishing the seven steps to cleaning the outside of the car, it is time to move inside the car. There are six major steps to cleaning the vehicle's interior.

Chunk 2 then follows.

Active Learning Opportunities

It is crucial to provide students with opportunities to reinforce the content we've presented. Kevin Kruse (2005) indicates that sensory storage processes all stimuli in real time, so as new information comes in, it replaces the previous information. These items will be held for only about thirty seconds unless a memory aid such as repetition or chunking is used. Research shows that the timing of these reinforcements is critical. Users have difficulty remembering even three elements after eighteen seconds. Further research has shown that the duration of short-term memory may be much shorter, decaying after about two seconds (Marsh, Sebrechts, Hicks, and Landau, 1997).

Both Softchalk and Respondus StudyMate allow creation of multiple learning activities during which students have an opportunity to spend more time on task, interact with the content, and reinforce the information in short-term memory. Each of these software packages provides an excellent return on investment for faculty time spent producing activities. For a single input of information, you can generate multiple exercises for your students.

Prioritizing Course Development and Revisions

Faculty are typically pressed for time and will not be able to chunk every module immediately, so you should select the highest-priority items for revision first. Here are some suggestions to consider when you are selecting your priority for chunking:

- Most student questions related to content
- Competency areas for which exam scores are lower
- Most difficult concepts
- Student complaints and comments
- You bore yourself with your own presentation

Evaluating the Effectiveness of Chunking

Your institution or department may have standardized evaluations, but a short questionnaire of two to five questions can elicit students' reaction to changes in the course and give you instant feedback about the effectiveness of the changes in length of presentations.

Action Steps

Step 20
Complete Form 9 for each major point.
> *Time estimate:* 1 to 3 hours

Step 21
Select one presentation, and find the breaks (electronically or on paper). Verify that you have a reinforcement activity for each chunk. Plan the introduction and transitions for each chunk. Use Form 10.
> *Time estimate:* 15 minutes

Step 22
Create chunks of content. Use the file and folder structures you have established to store these content files.
> *Time estimate:* 31 to 40 hours depending on how elaborate your product.

Design with
Process in Mind

Lesson Evaluation	
"Graded" assessments or evidence to proceed	• Ask peer to review course materials and be open to feedback about improvements.

It is important for you to develop a plan for progression through your course. Once you have all of the content developed, you will need to navigate through your course from the students' viewpoint. Is it clear how your Web-based course works? What is the overall pace or plan for students to proceed through the course? Will you have weekly discussions or assignments? What will a typical week be like for your students? What should they expect as far as time commitment, due dates, reading time? Students should be able to get an idea of the time commitment and frequency of projects, papers, and exams so that they are able to make a plan for working your course into the other aspects of their lives.

Best Practices

Develop a Schedule of Due Dates, and Stick to It

I learned to commit to dates at the beginning of the semester so that students can arrange work, child care, and other schedules. Showing my students this respect went a long way toward gaining much cooperation from them. I simply let them know that I understood they were juggling many aspects of their life. I wanted to respect and accommodate that as much as possible and still have education be a priority for them.

Keep Scheduling Convenience a Priority for Your Students

One of the main reasons your students are taking a Web-based course is convenience—not only for the convenience of not having to commute but for the scheduling convenience. If we as faculty then require synchronous sessions or multiple tests at monitored sites or tests with very short access time frames, we are negating the very reasons the students signed up for this course. If there are any such requirements as these, they should be stated prior to enrollment so students are not surprised and do not begin the semester feeling they have been misled.

I work in a health care center, and each patient has to sign an informed-consent form. Perhaps it would be helpful if we had something similar in education where students were informed about all of the factors in their course in advance and consent to those conditions prior to paying tuition.

Have Due Dates the Same Day Each Week

It is helpful to students if they are able to establish a routine with their lives: their families, work schedules, and study routines. If you typically have due dates on the same day of the week, this consistency will allow them to establish routines so they can meet their responsibilities. Allow students to get into a routine with their assignments and studying.

Be Consistent About Navigation

Have a course design that is consistent from module to module so students do not have to figure out each time where to go to get the assignments completed. The course is not a scavenger hunt.

Be Consistent About Where to Turn in Assignments

The same policy works here as for navigation. This is all common sense, so I know I needn't say it. It's just that some people get a bit bored with their course design and think being creative with navigation or assignment submissions or directions will keep the students on their toes. Students are more appreciative, though, when your creative energies are put toward making your content exciting. That's the part you can be the most effective at and the part they really need to remember the most.

Be Consistent About Your Availability

Develop a schedule of times you will answer questions, announce it to the class, and stick to it. You have to be careful about your own time and schedule. If you have not taught online before, it is tempting to be online seven days a week and to check in as soon as you wake up and just before you go to bed. I did that my first semester of teaching more out of nervousness because I was unsure of myself and how it was all going to work out. But it came back to haunt me after a while.

One Saturday evening a student posted a question at 10:45 P.M., and by 7:00 A.M. the next day (Sunday), I had a nasty message asking why I had not answered the question yet. It really wasn't the student's fault. They had all come to expect me to answer quickly (even though I suspected, and confirmed, that the student hadn't logged in again between those times) because I had been logging in at those times during the previous three to four weeks. I suddenly realized I wouldn't be sitting in my office between 10:45 P.M. Saturday and 7:00 a.m. Sunday in case a classroom student came by or called my office with a question and I hadn't suddenly gone to an around-the-clock job, so I shouldn't be that available for the online course either.

I needed to set parameters for student expectations and for my behavior about when I would take care of my online course. I set times for the students and myself and determined that I would answer questions posted after 4:00 by approximately 9:00 the next morning. Any questions posted during the day (after 9:00 A.M.) would be answered around 4:00 in the afternoon. The students therefore knew I was online Monday through Friday at 9:00 A.M. and 4:00 P.M. and took care of pending questions at those times. They also knew I would not be online on the weekends, so they needed to watch out for and help each other out on the weekends, during the day, and late at night. As long as they knew what to expect, things were fine, and I was also much better off.

Prioritize and Honor the Order in Which You Will Answer Messages from Students

Another communication management issue I learned is to prioritize the order in which I will answer messages from students. The priority worked best for me when I was reaching the greatest number of students.

I was also aware of trying to minimize communications with individual students unless it was for personal reasons, for two reasons. First, I did not want to become a personal tutor to twenty-five individual students, a highly inefficient use of time. Second, I wanted to be sure that all the students were getting the same information. I was concerned that I would teach one student something that the other students didn't receive the benefit of. I had some students who were too far away to meet with me, and I didn't want someone to have an unfair advantage just because he or she dropped by my office or called.

There were four means of communications coming from students:

- A discussion area or bulletin board where all the students could see the same information. This is the most efficient since everyone in the class sees it.

- E-mail within the course. This is the next most efficient because I choose when I get to read it.

- E-mail to my university account. This inserts itself into hundreds of other e-mails and has a tendency to get lost in the shuffle. I can't keep all course documents in one place

- Telephone calls. These are fine in an emergency situation.

This is the priority sequence I announced to the students and trained myself to be diligent in following it:

Discussion area. I explained that this is the quickest way to get in touch with me and that I always answer these questions first. So when I logged in at 9:00 A.M. and 4:00 P.M., I ignored the e-mail and went straight to the discussion area or bulletin board and answered those questions. I selected this discussion area first because this is the quickest way to the greatest number of students. Everyone in the class has the opportunity to get the information in this area.

E-mail within the course. After answering all the questions in the discussion area, I checked the course e-mail. If any of the questions in the e-mail pertained to content, I replied to the sender saying I'd received the e-mail and thought the question was of interest to the entire class. Therefore, the answer to the question would be in the discussion area/bulletin board, and I gave the message number. In this way, I redirected the students to the discussion area, pointing out that that is the place to get information about the course. I answer only personal or grade questions in e-mail.

E-mail to my work account. I told students that the only e-mail they should send to my office account is something of a technical nature (something is wrong with the server or the course) or there is a personal problem. If they are asking for course information, I reply to the e-mail asking them to log into the course and send this message as a discussion area message or an e-mail message, whichever is appropriate; I also refer them to the course syllabus, which gives those directions. I do not give them the information they are seeking. In addition, I will not reply to that e-mail until after I have answered all the messages in the discussion area of the course and the e-mails in the course.

Telephone calls to my office. These are almost always of a personal nature. If a call is not, I ask the student to first post the message on the bulletin board. If the student has already done this and is still having difficulty with the concept, then certainly a telephone call is in order. I even call the student later if this person indicates he or she is still having difficulty. I also inquire about the materials in the course and find out what wasn't clear and what might be helpful to make it clear to them.

These rules of prioritization on communication are more for me than the students. Nevertheless, the students adhere to them much better than I do. I want to jump every time one of them whimpers, but I have to remember that sometimes they figure it out on their own and sometimes they help each other figure it out, and these ways of learning are much better than my telling them.

I remember at the end of my master's program thanking my major professor for not being there every time I went down the hall to find him to answer a question. I was stuck and needed help, but when he wasn't there, I went back and struggled more and eventually worked many things out on my own. For others who are similarly overprotective, I think there are times when our students might benefit from a few chances to struggle with the content for a little while.

Create a "Coffee Shop" Forum for Social Interactions Among Students

We do not want to discourage the normal chitchat and social interactions that occur with students in a class; nevertheless, those do not need to happen during class or in a forum where other students are trying to get into the discussion area or bulletin board, do their assignment, and move on. It is fine for Vanessa to tell us where she went on spring break, but we do not want that message in with the messages we need to get through in order to get our assignments completed.

Communicate an Appropriate Pace for Working Through the Course

One system I found helpful was to set due dates in advance. I told the students that it was fine for them to work ahead, but they could not work behind. This is especially important if you are having discussion questions in the discussion area. It is not easy to "discuss" with only one other person and impossible if the student is the only one in the discussion area during a certain time period because he or she is working ahead or behind the rest of the class members. Even if there is flexible entry and exit, it might be possible to group students into cohorts based on their entry dates or pace.

Discussion Assignments Must Give Students a Specific Item on Which to Comment

We need to distinguish between discussion questions for the discussion area and paragraph or essay-type questions on an exam. Essay or paragraph questions have one correct answer, often with multiple points to the answer. If those same questions are placed in a Web-based course and the students are told to "discuss," it will be very difficult to get interaction. After the first person presents the correct answer and the second person rewords it to say the same or a similar thing but in different words, what will the remainder of the students have to write? At that point, the remaining students are limited to "I agree," "I think that is a good point," "I disagree because . . .," and other similar limited response questions.

Good discussion questions elicit discussion. It helps if you can have students bring in their own experience and expertise to exemplify concepts. An additional option is to assign students a role to play in the discussion of a particular topic. Workable roles include pro and con stance, the summarizer for the group, and the questioner who asks for clarification. Another technique is to assign roles based on stakeholders in the scenario you have presented. For example, when presenting a case in which a controversial pesticide is being used, stakeholders might include the farmer, nearby home owners, other competing farmers in the area, the seed company, the company selling the pesticide, consumers of the food being produced, grocery stores supplied by the farmer, extension personnel, and many more. In a hospital scenario, stakeholders could include physicians, nurses, the patient, family members of the patient, hospital staff, the billing office, the medical supplies department, and the pharmacy.

It is sometimes difficult to get a group of people to each "tell us something about yourself," but if instead you say, "Tell us your name, where you are from, your major and if you have pets, what kind," it makes it much easier for people to tell something about themselves because you have given them specifics to address. So it is often in a discussion area when you present a question, even a controversial one, and want people to engage in discussion. It is much easier if you tell them something to talk about. For example, you might ask students to present a lesson plan on a particular topic. The follow-up instructions might be to reply to at least one of the other students with a positive suggestion about how to improve their lesson plan.

In addition, it is vital to have a deadline on first posts if a second post is expected during the week. Otherwise most students might wait until the night of the deadline to make the first posts and then other students cannot complete their assignment because their colleagues have procrastinated. So you might make first posts due on Wednesday at noon and follow-ups due by Friday at midnight or a similar schedule that fits the pace of progression in the course.

Design Using Someone Else's Mind

It is now time for you to ask someone else to look over your course materials. If your institution does not have a peer review process in place, you may want to begin one by informally asking another colleague to review your materials. This process will eventually catch on.

Many of us think what happens in the classroom is sacred and between us and the students and that, as a bumper sticker I saw stated so eloquently, "What you think of me is none of my business!" However, we have been working on these materials long and hard, and it is difficult at this point to find any errors or typos or even things which may be unclear because you wrote it and you know what you meant to say. I promise it will save you time during the semester if you have someone else look it over now and find all those little issues for you rather than fifteen to fifty students each finding and pointing it out during the semester, so then you have to scramble and find a way to fix it fast.

In addition, a Web-based course is much more like a published article than a lecture you may give. We call these this Web-based content "enduring materials." They are right there in black and white (or bright blue and white) for everyone to see on the screen. You want to present your best work.

If this is the first time you have offered the course, you may be amazed at the misinterpretations that result. Instructions that seem perfectly clear to you will be misinterpreted in surprising ways.

While your course is being reviewed, take an opportunity to recognize all the work you have accomplished throughout the last five chapters. This is a good time to congratulate yourself and take a momentary break from your Web-based course development until the reviews are returned.

Action Step

Step 23

Develop a naming scheme for the assignments themselves and for the files you create for students to download. In addition, you will need to tell the students what to name the file when they turn it in to you. You don't need thirty-five Assignment01.doc files in your folder. The assignment tool in WebCT will download the file as the student's name. If you are having students submit assignments by e-mail or the discussion area or any other way, they will need specific instructions about how to name that assignment.

Time estimate: None if you use the suggestion I propose; 30 to 45 minutes if you create your own

Design with Navigation in Mind

Learning Goals/Outcomes	
Development of learning guides	Upon completion of this chapter, the faculty member will: • Be aware uploading course materials is one of the last tasks for conquering the content. • Place all components of one module on a single page to provide clarity for student navigation. • Identify next steps for proceeding with Web-based courses.

Learning Resources	
Required resources	Chapter 7 *Conquering the Content*
Additional resources	None

Learning Activities	
Activities for this lesson	• Customize call log for your course. • Begin to upload course materials. • Make final decisions needed before course will be offered online.

Self-Assessment	
Check your understanding	• Completed course documents • Determine answers to questions about next steps in course development

Lesson Evaluation	
"Graded" assessments or evidence to proceed	• The content has been conquered!

Navigation is so close to the end of this process because putting course materials into the course management system before completing those materials will cause extra work. Editing after files are already in the system means you will need to edit offline and re-upload files at best. At worst, you may have to rebuild portions of the course online. There are some easy html editors that allow you to preview your lessons with one click of the mouse so that you do not have to move them into a course management system in order to see what your lessons will look like online. Softchalk allows you to embed reinforcement activities directly into the lessons so that you can review and reinforce concepts as you teach them. Remember to seal the concepts with an activity.

Student Access to Module Components

It is very helpful if students are able to navigate to all components of a module from one page in the course. All navigation pertaining to Module 1 will originate from a single page so that students are not searching around the learning management system for the tasks to be completed. It may make sense to you to group all videos under one icon, all study guides under another, and so forth. However, when students log in to the course to complete a lesson, it is much easier for them to complete what they need to for an individual lesson if everything is on one page. Although you may have everything they need to complete listed on the learning guide, it is still important to have tasks grouped on one page so that students are not spending needless time navigating about the course rather than spending their time focusing on course content.

Remember that the learning guide includes all the components for a module, so you may take the major topics on the learning guide and create a table of contents based on this list. Naturally there will be multiple components of the presentation of content and concepts; these are the chunks you have produced.

Continuous Improvement

You will be making revisions to your course in the future. If you've followed the system in this book, everything is well formatted for you to make those revisions easily. During the first semester you teach, you will notice parts of the course that don't work the way you envisioned. This is to be expected, so do not be dismayed when this occurs. Perhaps what I wrote didn't come across to you exactly as I meant it, or perhaps your teaching style is a bit different or your course materials or the students you are dealing with require alterations. All of these will cause you to need to customize your individual courses to fit your own needs. In addition, I don't know the environment at your institution; it has its own unique policies, regulations, or politics that need to be followed in order for you to blend into your environment.

I will suggest several documents for you to keep at hand so you can be opportunistic about keeping records on your observations. Then when it is time to update your course, you will have all the information you need in one place.

The call log (Form 9) is the most comprehensive of these documents; it allows you to develop course revisions based on learning outcomes and student need. You may not have time to revise everything you want to after the first semester of teaching, so it is important to prioritize these revisions based on increasing performance on learning outcomes.

You document telephone calls for assistance on the call log sequentially as calls or concerns arise. There are multiple purposes for documenting these calls. First, you note the number of student calls you are receiving. With this information documented, you are equipped to show your supervisor the volume of student interactions in which you are involved even though you are not "meeting class"; track "high maintenance" students (those students who require an inordinate amount of your time, register late, request make-up exams, miss deadlines, and just don't have it all together yet); and ascertain how students fare in your course depending on their computer and reading skill levels.

Second, the call log points to portions of the course in which issues occur based on student learning styles. Log the learning styles of students and portions of the course where issues occur; the frequency of calls for individual students; and the time on task for you based on student learning styles and particular portions of your Web-based course. From this information, you can determine whether the issues are logistical and related to a need for clarification of directions, processes, and increased computer skills or concept related, with a need to clarify concepts, provide background information, or offer additional learning exercises. The call log will also reveal whether visual, auditory, kinesthetic, read-write, or global explanations of your course are lacking depending on the frequency of calls from students with these learning styles in each component of your course.

With the call log, you can track the amount of time you are spending during the semester solving problems in your course. You also can track "high-maintenance" students. Documentation can help you discover if your interventions are making a difference, or if students taking an inordinate amount of your time eventually drop and prove to be a drain on the time you are available to spend with other students who progress through the course. Check for correlations between these students and students who enrolled late but within institutional deadlines, were allowed to bend the rules on prerequisites for entry into your course, do not have a computer at home, or were allowed to enter the course beyond normal institutional enrollment deadlines and each of these situations compared to students who eventually drop the course. The call log is in the format of an Excel spreadsheet or MSWord table that lists several columns of information.

Documenting for Revisions

Categories to Document

During each semester of your Web-based course, keep a record of the things that need attention in your course prior to the next time it is taught. It is much easier to note these along the way rather than trying to think back through it all during the busyness of the next semester. Here are the categories I've found helpful in updating courses.

FAQ Keeping a list of FAQs for your course is a way to reduce your time on task yet still provide answers to students' questions. You may want to have two FAQ lists: one on course procedures and another on content. You may update these documents as the need arises. I've found it helpful to make an announcement of the answer in the discussion area when I first compose it. If it was not in the list of FAQs at the beginning of the course, then I add it to the FAQ file, and it will be available from that point forward, including the beginning of the next semester.

List of Issues and Revisions As issues arise during the semester, it will be convenient if you compile them in one file. As you record each issue, if you have an idea about how to revise the course to alleviate this concern, record it alongside the issue. With these issues and ideas gathered conveniently in one place, it will be much more efficient for you to make the changes to improve your course for the following semester.

Suggestions During your course, students may make suggestions about it. Do not view these suggestions as criticism; rather, it is useful information for you. I usually tell students when they are the pioneers for the online version of the course and say that any suggestions they can make about the course will be welcome and can benefit students who take the course in the future.

Students have a unique perspective on your course that you cannot match, no matter how many times you review the course. One of your goals is that your course be as effective as possible, and students can go a long way toward assisting you with this goal. I've found students are eager to assist and usually provide valuable assistance for course revisions. You may have to distinguish between comments that are attempts to increase grades versus comments that are truly constructive, but most faculty members recognize this difference. Asking for suggestions provides an additional opportunity for you to show respect to your students, which in turn typically garners a favorable view of you as an instructor.

Blog or Journal of Your Experiences It is to my great regret that I did not write my experiences in a journal the first few semesters I taught online. I did several comparisons between Web-based and face-to-face courses during my first four to six semesters of teaching. A record of my own observations, recorded during the experience, would be valuable to me now. This blog or journal may become an entry in your teaching portfolio and can also give you important insights about teaching and learning as your skills progress.

One experience I remember well is that I taught both a Web-based course and a classroom course at the same time. I gave both groups of students access to both modes of delivery. I thought that the online students would want to come to class in order to get real-time demonstrations and an opportunity to get the information in person. To my great surprise, it was the classroom students who wanted access to the Web-based materials, and not a single student taking the Web-based course ever came to a classroom session. I suppose I could have taken this as an indictment of my teaching presence, but my optimistic outlook led me to the conclusion it was due to the value and convenience of the Web-based materials. In fact, this view was supported by student evaluations of the courses at the end of the semester. I mentioned earlier my realization that use of the learning guides online and the experience of revising my course organization as a whole changed my classroom teaching for the better.

I am certain there were many other valuable experiences that could provide similar insights had I taken the time to record them. It is common among faculty teaching online to experience lessons valuable to their teaching. Evidence of these experiences in a journal will provide you with a record of your growth as an instructor and can benefit those of us who are continually learning from sharing each other's teaching experiences. It may also surprise you how much your teaching skills are advanced by the experience of teaching a Web-based course. And what teacher doesn't benefit from a positive achievement?

Items to Document

- Concepts that were difficult or which test or assignment questions caused difficulty

- It is beneficial to prepare for course revisions and updates during the first semester you teach your Web-based course. Once again it will be important to prioritize the revisions to be made before teaching your course for the second time. The highest priority revisions will be those that have an effect on student outcomes. Documenting the following items will assist in your determining the priority revisions.

- Discussion questions that needed clarification

- Assignments that needed more explicit instructions, alterations, or changed grading

- Assignment rubrics that may not have worked well

- Quiz questions with issues, for example, poor wording or answer choices or incorrect number of points assigned

- Project feedback from students

- Updates for presentations or text-based content

- Updates on content for current events

If you have feedback you give frequently for assignments, consider keeping a file of these explanations so you can copy and paste without having to recreate this information each time. An example might be an explanation on the use of adverbs and adjectives for written papers.

This list seems like a lot to document, but it can be easy to do. I keep a file on my desktop to record this information so that with one mouse click, I am into the file and typing my ideas.

Saving mouse clicks is always a goal of mine. Multiple mouse clicks may take only a couple of extra seconds, but with Web-based learning, a couple of extra seconds adds up in hundreds of places and quickly turns into minutes and hours.

Link Rot

Link rot is just what it sounds like, and when your links rot, you need to know. Web sites are updated often, so you need a system to check those links periodically. Typically links will be scattered throughout your course at the places students will need to access them. You don't want to lose the design of students having all their materials where they need them, but it is not efficient for you to go through the entire course page by page searching for links to check and see if they still work. It is also not very professional to wait until the break and let the students tell you there are rotten links in your course.

I have an efficient and convenient way of ensuring your course does not become infested with link rot. Use Form 12 to paste every link in the course (preferably as you create each) and also note the location of the link within the module, topic, and chunk. Then once a month or so, open the spreadsheet and click on each URL to find out if it is still working. For any that are no longer current, find the updated link, log it on the form, and then go directly to the course content where it is listed and replace the URL.

Where to Go from Here

In spite of all of the information in this book, there is still more to learn. Two topics are of major interest: the learning management system and facilitating an online course.

Learning Management System

One of the things you will need to tackle is getting your content into your learning or course management system. You may be using Blackboard (some products formerly WebCT), Moodle, Desire2Learn, Angel, or a home-grown system, but whatever that system is, you'll need to request a course shell and obtain a login and password to access the course you will be developing.

That works in different ways on different campuses, so you'll have to find the appropriate person to talk with at your institution and how that permission is given. Some institutions expect the faculty to upload course materials themselves; others have people who input the course materials for the faculty (this is less common). If you need to develop the course yourself, you may be required to go through a training or certification course before you are allowed to teach with that system. Therefore, investigate the policies on your campus for Web-based learning faculty.

Facilitating a Web-Based Course

In Chapter Six, I addressed managing student communication and other issues that will come into play as you are teaching. I did not fully address facilitating group discussions, collaborative learning, or group work, and those sorts of issues that will be something you will want to learn more about depending on the way you will be running your course. I suggest consulting several good references—for example:

Conrad, R., and Donaldson, J. *Engaging the Online Learner: Activities and Resources for Creative Instruction.* San Francisco: Jossey-Bass, 2004.

Palloff, R., and Pratt, K. *Collaborating Online: Learning Together in Community.* San Francisco: Jossey-Bass, 2005.

Palloff, R., and Pratt, K. *Building Online Communities: Effective Strategies for the Virtual Classroom.* San Francisco: Jossey-Bass, 2007.

Weimer, M. *Learner-Centered Teaching: Five Key Changes to Practice.* San Francisco: Jossey-Bass, 2002.

Action Steps

Step 24

Customize Form 11, the Call Log. Create a spreadsheet form on your desktop to document student phone calls, student learning styles, and issues with your course.

Time estimate: 25 minutes if you do it before the semester begins; 90 minutes if you do it after the semester begins

Step 25

Create a link rot form like that in Form 12.

Time estimate: 10 to 15 minutes to set up the form; then a minimal amount of time if you record the links as you create them

What You Have Conquered

Take a look at how far you've come since you started this book. You have accomplished a tremendous amount and should be pleased with your progress. After school starts, you will be relieved that you have put in this much preparation time in advance of the start of the semester.

Now take an opportunity to congratulate yourself and celebrate your accomplishments. If you are still reading at this point, that means you are definitely a conqueror!

Thank you for making the journey with me. I would love to know about the course you have developed or are in the process of developing. Please shoot me an e-mail and let me know you made it to the end of the book and what subject matter you are teaching: smithrobinm@uams.edu. I look forward to hearing you have conquered the content.

Forms

This appendix contains the forms you will need for the action steps in this book. These forms provide the structure you need to develop your course in a simple, stepwise manner, and they will therefore free you from disorganization and from not knowing what to do next. You will need multiple copies of some forms to complete your course development.[*]

Some people benefit from an organization scheme that keeps them grounded. Others feel oppressed by forms. If you despise forms and are able to organize yourself in another way, skip the forms. If the forms are a hindrance rather than a help, take the ideas from the reading and put them into practice in your own style.

---

[*] Forms are for individual use only.

Form 1: My Favorite Teacher

The subject this person taught

The year in school I had this teacher:

The main thing that comes to mind when I think of this teacher:

What he or she did that caught my attention:

The qualities that stand out about his or her teaching:

Form 2: Course Content:
Current Organization of Course

Course title: _____

2A: Course Evaluation Measures: Course Tests

Current Test	*Content Covered*	*Notes*

2B: Course Evaluation Measures: Current Quizzes/Assignments

Quiz or Assignment	Content Covered	Notes

2C: Course Assessment Measures: Current Major Projects and Other Assignments

Major Project	Project Topic	Notes

Assignment	Content Covered	Notes

Form 3: Course Revision Thoughts

Things that are working well in my course

Things that I'd like to change about my course

The most frustrating or irritating aspect of my course is:

-
-
-
-

The most time-consuming aspect of my course is:

-
-

Form 4: Converting Chapters to Topics

List the sequence of chapters used in your course.

Before Course Revision

Chapter _____
Chapter _____
Chapter _____
Chapter _____
Chapter _____
Chapter _____
Chapter _____
Chapter _____
Chapter _____
Chapter _____
Chapter _____
Chapter _____
Chapter _____
Chapter _____
Chapter _____
Chapter _____

List the sequence of chapters and the topics those chapters represent

After Course Revision

Chapter _____ = _____
Chapter _____ = _____
Chapter _____ = _____
Chapter _____ = _____
Chapter _____ = _____
Chapter _____ = _____
Chapter _____ = _____
Chapter _____ = _____

Chapter _____ = _____

Chapter _____ = _____

Chapter _____ = _____

Chapter _____ = _____

Chapter _____ = _____

Chapter _____ = _____

Chapter _____ = _____

Chapter _____ = _____

Form 4 Sample

Before Course Revision

Chapter 1
Chapter 2
Chapter 3
Chapter 4
Chapter 5
Chapter 6
Chapter 7

•

•

•

Chapter 31
Chapter 30

After Course Revision

Chapter 31 = Biomes
Chapter 30 = Ecosystems
Chapter 1 = Life
Chapter 2 = Characteristics of Living Things
Chapter 3= Cells
Chapter 4 = Organelles
Chapter 5 = Cell processes
Chapter 6 = Photosynthesis
Chapter 7 = Cellular respiration

Form 5: Documenting the Web-Based Course

Course name_____

Course Learning Modules:

#	Module Title
1	
2	
3	
4	
5	
6	
7	
8	
9	
10	
11	
12	
13	
14	
15	

These module names will be used to populate the first column of Form 6.

Form 6: Course Outline

Course title: _____

Module Number and Name	Competency/Outcome
1	1
	2
	3
	4
	5
	6
	7

Module Number and Name	Competency/Outcome
2	1
	2
	3
	4
	5
	6
	7

Module Number and Name	Competency/Outcome
3	1
	2
	3
	4
	5
	6
	7

Module Number and Name	Competency/Outcome
4	1
	2
	3
	4
	5
	6
	7

Form 6: Course Outline

Course title: _____

Module Number and Name	Competency/Outcome
5	1
	2
	3
	4
	5
	6
	7
Module Number and Name	*Competency/Outcome*
6	1
	2
	3
	4
	5
	6
	7
Module Number and Name	*Competency/Outcome*
7	1
	2
	3
	4
	5
	6
	7
Module Number and Name	*Competency/Outcome*
8	1
	2
	3
	4
	5
	6
	7

Form 6: Course Outline

Course title: _____

Module Number and Name	Competency/Outcome	
9	1	
	2	
	3	
	4	
	5	
	6	
	7	

Module Number and Name	Competency/Outcome	
10	1	
	2	
	3	
	4	
	5	
	6	
	7	

Module Number and Name	Competency/Outcome	
11	1	
	2	
	3	
	4	
	5	
	6	
	7	

Module Number and Name	Competency/Outcome	
12	1	
	2	
	3	
	4	
	5	
	6	
	7	

Form 6: Course Outline

Course title: _____

Module Number and Name	Competency/Outcome
13	1
	2
	3
	4
	5
	6
	7

Module Number and Name	Competency/Outcome
14	1
	2
	3
	4
	5
	6
	7

Module Number and Name	Competency/Outcome
15	1
	2
	3
	4
	5
	6
	7

Form 7: Learning Process

Course Name: _____

Module Name: _____

Competency: _____

Major Point: _____

How will I know if my niece or nephew knows this?

Best ways for my niece or nephew to learn this:

   Experiences:

   People to see:

   Places to go (may be virtual):

   Things to read:

   Things to talk about:

Form 8: Course Outline with Competencies and Major Outcomes

Module Number	Competency/Outcome	Major Points
1	1	1
		2
		3
		4
		5
		6
		7
	2	1
		2
		3
		4
		5
		6
		7
	3	1
		2
		3
		4
		5
		6
		7
	4	1
		2
		3
		4
		5
		6
		7

Form 8

Number	Competency/Outcome	Major Points	
	5	1	
		2	
		3	
		4	
		5	
		6	
		7	
	6	1	
		2	
		3	
		4	
		5	
		6	
		7	
	7	1	
		2	
		3	
		4	
		5	
		6	
		7	
	8	1	
		2	
		3	
		4	
		5	
		6	
		7	

Form 9: Learning Guide

Module Name:
Course Name:

Learning Goals/Outcomes

Upon completion of this module, the student will be able to:

-
-
-

Learning Resources

Required Resources

-
-
-

Additional Resources

-
-
-

Learning Activities

Activities for This Lesson

-
-
-
-

Discussion Questions

-
-
-
-

Self-Assessment
Check Your Understanding

-
-
-
-

Lesson Evaluation: Graded Assessments

-
-
-

Form 10: Chunks and Bridges

Chunk	Reinforcement Activity	Introduction/Transition
Title for content chunk	Record interactive learning opportunity for this chunk	Introduction to Chunk Content Chunk Transition to the next chunk

Chunk 1	Reinforcement Activity	Introduction/Transition
		Content Chunk

Chunk 2	Reinforcement Activity	Introduction/Transition
		Content Chunk

Chunk 3	Reinforcement Activity	Introduction/Transition
		Content Chunk

Chunk 4	Reinforcement Activity	Introduction/Transition
		Content Chunk

Conquering the Content by Robin M. Smith. Copyright © 2008 John Wiley and Sons, Inc.

Chunk 5	Reinforcement Activity	Introduction/Transition
		Content Chunk

Chunk 6	Reinforcement Activity	Introduction/Transition
		Content Chunk

Chunk 7	Reinforcement Activity	Introduction/Transition
		Content Chunk

Chunk 8	Reinforcement Activity	Introduction/Transition
		Content Chunk

Chunk 9	Reinforcement Activity	Introduction/Transition
		Content Chunk

Surround each of those concepts with an introduction and reinforcement plus a transition to the next concept. This gives each concept some context so that they are not just isolated ideas, so students will have some understanding of how all of these concepts are interrelated.

Take a look at the material left over after you extract these portions of your lecture. Ask yourself what value is added by that content? If your arch enemy on campus could justify to you there are pedagogical reasons to use this material in his or her course, then use it. If not, perhaps you need to question why you plan to leave it in.

Form 11: Call Log

Course Name: _____ Semester: _____

Date	Learning Style	Student Name	Topic	Sect.	Question	Issues	Notes

Form 12: Link Rot

Course Name: _____ Semester: _____ Last Updated: _____

Working URL	Content Module	LG or Module #	LG Element	Competency
http://www .acponline.org/ ethics/ethicman .htm#informed	Informed Consent	1	Introduction	References
http://www .ama-assn.org/ ama/pub/ category/ 4608.html	Informed Consent	Physician Laws		Content
http://griffi n.med.drexel .edu/MedEthEx/ index.html	Informed Consent	Ethical Conduct		References

Action Steps

Chapter One

1. Select one course to develop as you progress through this book. Reflect on your favorite teachers in the past and the positive qualities that made them memorable using Form 1.

2. Gather all materials for the entire semester you've used in the past to teach the course.

3. Document the way the course is currently organized (grades, quizzes, projects, exams) using Forms 2A, 2B, and 2C.

4. Document your thoughts on course revisions using Form 3.

5. Preview online content. Use Ideas for Application in Chapter One to record your observations.

6. Document in Form 4 the modules you will cover over the entire duration of the course.

Chapter Two

7. Using Form 5, transfer and verify the topics you identified on the bottom of Form 4. This will finalize the module names for your Web-based course. Use Form 7.

8. Make a folder for one module on your computer's hard drive.

9. Make a subfolder within the folder you made in step 8 for each component of the learning guide for which you will have multiple files. Label each so you will know it belongs to Module01.

10. Copy the folder and subfolder structure you just created, and paste it into the main course folder enough times to have a set of folders and subfolders for each of your modules.

11. On Form 6, record the five to seven highest priority competencies for each module.

12. Select five to seven major points within which to organize the content for each competency, and record these on Form 8. Repeat this step for each of the modules for your course.

Chapter Three

13. If it were up to you for your favorite niece or nephew to learn that first outcome in your course, what would be the best way she or he could learn that lesson? Write this information down on Form 7.

14. Repeat this process for each of the major points or outcomes for your course.

15. Translate each of the points in step 14 into the Web-based environment.

16. Plan assessments for learning outcomes for each module.

17. Develop assessment and evaluation documents for each module.

Chapter Four

18. Create objectives or learning outcomes for each module and record these on Form 9. Use the competencies you've provided on Form 6 to create the learning outcomes.

19. Complete the learning guide for each module in the course.

Chapter Five

20. Complete 9 for each major point.

Repeat steps 11 to 20 for each module.

After completing all of the learning guides for the entire course, prioritize in order to make the best use of the time available between now and the beginning of the semester. In most cases, there will not be time to develop all the content and all the learning resources for the Web-based course prior to the first time it is taught. Therefore, here are two questions to consider in determining the items to address first:

- What is the most irritating aspect of your course?
- What is the most time-consuming aspect of your course?

Either of these areas will provide a high return on investment for your time.

After making these decisions, proceed with the remainder of the steps for your priority segments. Then proceed with steps 21 to 25 for the balance of the segments.

21. Select one presentation and find the breaks (electronically or on paper). Verify that you have a reinforcement activity for each chunk. Plan the introduction and transitions for each chunk. Use Form 10.
22. Create the actual chunks of content.

Chapter Six

23. Develop a naming scheme for the assignments and the files you create for students to download.

Chapter Seven

24. Customize the call log in Form 11.
25. Develop a link rot form like that in Form 12.

American Association for Higher Education's Nine Principles of Good Practice for Assessing Student Learning

1. *The assessment of student learning begins with educational values.* Assessment is not an end in itself but a vehicle for educational improvement. Its effective practice, then, begins with and enacts a vision of the kinds of learning we most value for students and strive to help them achieve. Educational values should drive not only *what* we choose to assess but also *how* we do so. Where questions about educational mission and values are skipped over, assessment threatens to

This was written by Alexander W. Astin; Trudy W. Banta; K. Patricia Cross; Elaine El-Khawas; Peter T. Ewell; Pat Hutchings; Theodore J. Marchese; Kay M. McClenney; Marcia Mentkowski; Margaret A. Miller; E. Thomas Moran; and Barbara D. Wright. This document was developed under the auspices of the AAHE Assessment Forum with support from the Fund for the Improvement of Postsecondary Education with additional support for publication and dissemination from the Exxon Education Foundation. Copies may be made without restriction. Printed with permission by the publisher. Stylus Publishing, LLC. This material is also available online at http:/styluspub.com/books/AAHEPGP.pdf be an exercise in measuring what's easy, rather than a process of improving what we really care about.

2. *Assessment is most effective when it reflects an understanding of learning as multidimensional, integrated, and revealed in performance over time.* Learning is a complex process. It entails not only what students know but what they can do with what they know; it involves not only knowledge and abilities but values, attitudes, and habits of mind that affect both academic success and performance beyond the classroom. Assessment should reflect these understandings by employing a diverse array of methods, including those that call for actual performance, using them over time so as to reveal change, growth, and increasing degrees of integration. Such an approach aims for a more complete and accurate picture of learning, and therefore firmer bases for improving our students' educational experience.

3. *Assessment works best when the programs it seeks to improve have clear, explicitly stated purposes.* Assessment is a goal-oriented process. It entails comparing educational performance with educational purposes and expectations—those derived from the institution's mission, from faculty intentions in program and course design, and from knowledge of students' own goals. Where program purposes lack specificity or agreement, assessment as a process pushes a campus toward clarity about where to aim and what standards to apply; assessment also prompts attention to where and how program goals will be taught and learned. Clear, shared, implementable goals are the cornerstone for assessment that is focused and useful.

4. *Assessment requires attention to outcomes but also and equally to the experiences that lead to those outcomes.* Information about outcomes is of high importance; where students "end up" matters greatly. But to improve outcomes, we need to know about student experience along the way—about the curricula, teaching, and kind of student effort that lead to particular outcomes. Assessment can help us understand which students learn best under what conditions; with such knowledge comes the capacity to improve the whole of their learning.

5. *Assessment works best when it is ongoing, not episodic.* Assessment is a process whose power is cumulative. Though isolated, "one-shot" assessment can be better than none, improvement is best fostered when assessment entails a linked series of activities undertaken over time. This may mean tracking the process of individual students, or of cohorts of students; it may mean collecting the same exam-

ples of student performance or using the same instrument semester after semester. The point is to monitor progress toward intended goals in a spirit of continuous improvement. Along the way, the assessment process itself should be evaluated and refined in light of emerging insights.

6. *Assessment fosters wider improvement when representatives from across the educational community are involved.* Student learning is a campus-wide responsibility, and assessment is a way of enacting that responsibility. Thus, while assessment efforts may start small, the aim over time is to involve people from across the educational community. Faculty play an especially important role, but assessment's questions can't be fully addressed without participation by student-affairs educators, librarians, administrators, and students. Assessment may also involve individuals from beyond the campus (alumni/ae, trustees, employers) whose experience can enrich the sense of appropriate aims and standards for learning. Thus understood, assessment is not a task for small groups of experts but a collaborative activity; its aim is wider, better-informed attention to student learning by all parties with a stake in its improvement.

7. *Assessment makes a difference when it begins with issues of use and illuminates questions that people really care about.* Assessment recognizes the value of information in the process of improvement. But to be useful, information must be connected to issues or questions that people really care about. This implies assessment approaches that produce evidence that relevant parties will find credible, suggestive, and applicable to decisions that need to be made. It means thinking in advance about how the information will be used, and by whom. The point of assessment is not to gather data and return "results"; it is a process that starts with the questions of decision-makers, that involves them in the gathering and interpreting of data, and that informs and helps guide continuous improvement.

8. *Assessment is most likely to lead to improvement when it is part of a larger set of conditions that promote change.* Assessment alone changes little. Its greatest contribution comes on campuses where the quality of teaching and learning is visibly valued and worked at. On such campuses, the push to improve educational performance is a visible and primary goal of leadership; improving the quality of undergraduate education is central to the institution's planning, budgeting, and personnel decisions. On such campuses, information about learning outcomes is seen as an integral part of decision making, and avidly sought.

9. *Through assessment, educators meet responsibilities to students and to the public.* There is a compelling public stake in education. As educators, we have a responsibility to the publics that support or depend on us to provide information about the ways in which our students meet goals and expectations. But that responsibility goes beyond the reporting of such information; our deeper obligation—to ourselves, our students, and society—is to improve. Those to whom educators are accountable have a corresponding obligation to support such attempts at improvement.

Design and Development Tasks

The following design and development tasks should be completed before the semester begins. This is not an exhaustive list, but it captures the majority of the tasks.

Learning Guide

- Develop learning guides, and convert them to html format.
- Upload these guides.

Content

- Develop lessons, for example, information discovery exercises, information presentations, exploratory adventures to seek out information, collaborative hunts, and guided learning experiences. Convert them to html format or other format suitable for a browser to read.

Activities

- Develop lesson interaction opportunities.
- Link lesson interaction opportunities.
- Determine a grading system for the lesson interaction opportunities.
- Upload lesson files.

- Link lesson files to appropriate pages in the course management system or the learning management system.

Quiz Questions

- Determine a naming scheme for quiz questions that makes it possible to identify the module, the topic, and question alternates.
- Develop quiz questions.
- Develop question alternates.
- Develop a naming convention for question. alternates so they are easy to recognize.
- Upload questions for quizzes.
- Create question sets.

Quiz Creation

- Create quizzes.
- Determine point values for quiz questions.

Quiz Settings

- Link quizzes to module pages.
- Determine release information for quiz results.
- Determine availability dates for quizzes.
- Determine if quizzes will be timed.
- If using a secure browser, create a password and instructions for students.

Discussion

- Formulate discussion questions.
- Formulate follow-up question for each discussion question.
- Determine the timing sequence of questions and follow-up questions.
- Design a rubric for discussions, and convert it to html format.
- Upload the rubric for discussions.

- Link the rubric for discussions to the module page.
- Determine point assignments for discussions.
- Create discussion topics.
- Determine whether group assignments will be made for discussions.
- Determine the design for group assignments.
- Create groups.

Assignments

- Develop assignments, and convert them to html format.
- Develop forms or documents for students to download for assignments.
- Create assignments.
- Determine point values for assignments.
- Provide explicit instructions for assignments.
- Upload the assignment files.
- Develop a grading rubric for each assignment, and convert each to html format.
- Upload the grading rubric for all assignments.

Syllabus

- Develop a grading system for the course.
- Create a syllabus, and convert it to html format.
- Upload the syllabus if it was not created with course management system tools.
- Link the syllabus.

Course Policies

- Create course policies, and convert them to html format.
- Link course policies.
- Create an introduction to the course, and convert it to html format.
- Upload the introduction to the course.
- Link the introduction to the course.

Calendar

- Develop a schedule for the course.
- Create calendar entries that match the schedule.
- Ensure that calendar entries, assignment due dates, quiz dates. and discussion dates correspond.

Learning Resources

- Create links to learning resources in the course.
- Seek permission for copyright clearance as necessary for learning resources.

Course Design

- Make certain the course navigation is clear and consistent.
- Remove any unused icons on the home page or within any other navigation tools.
- Ensure that naming schemes are consistent throughout the course.
- Have the course peer-reviewed.
- Make changes as needed following the peer review.

Link Rot

- Check for link rot (see Form 12 in Appendix A).
- Update rotten links.

Notes:
Ideas for Application

Chapter One: Design with Learning in Mind

Chapter Two: Design with the Future in Mind

Chapter Three: Design with Assessment in Mind

Chapter Four: Design with Organization in Mind

Chapter Five: Design with Content in Mind

Chapter Six: Design with Process in Mind

Chapter Seven: Design with Navigation in Mind

References

American Association of Higher Education Assessment Forum. *AAHE's Principles of Good Practice for Assessing Student Learning,* 1992. Also at http://styluspub.com/books/AAHEPGP.pdf

Awalt, C. "Speaking Personally—with Tony Bates." *American Journal of Distance Education,* 2007, *21*(2), 105–109.

Boettcher, J. "Ten Core Principles for Designing Effective Learning Environments: Insights from Brain Research and Pedagogical Theory." *Innovate,* 2007, *3*(3). http://www.Innovateonline.info/index.php?view=article&id=54.

Chandler, P., and Sweller, J. "The Split-Attention Effect as a Factor in the Design of Instruction." *British Journal of Educational Psychology,* 1992, *62*(2), 233–246.

Chickering, A., and Ehrmann, S. "Implementing the Seven Principles: Technology as Lever." *AAHE Bulletin,* October 1996, pp. 3–6.

Chickering, A., and Gamson, Z. "Seven Principles for Good Practice in Undergraduate Education." *AAHE Bulletin,* Mar. 1987, pp. 3–6.

Clark, R. C., Nguyen, F., and Sweller, J. *Efficiency in Learning: Evidence-Based Guidelines to Manage Cognitive Load.* San Francisco: Jossey-Bass/Pfeiffer, 2006.

Comeaux, P. *Assessing Online Learning.* San Francisco: Jossey-Bass, 2005.

Conrad, R., and Donaldson, J. *Engaging the Online Learner: Activities and Resources for Creative Instruction.* San Francisco: Jossey-Bass, 2004.

Cook, M. P. *"Visual Representations in Science Education: The Influence of Prior Knowledge and Cognitive Load Theory on Instructional Design Principles."* Science Education, 90(6) 1073–1091, 2006.

Denman, M. "How to Create Memorable Lectures." *Newsletter on Teaching,* Center for Teaching and Learning, Stanford University, Winter 2005, *14*(1), 1–5.

Draves, W. A. *Teaching Online* (2nd ed.). River Falls, Wis.: Learning Resources Network, 2002.

Felder, R. "Learning and Teaching Styles in Engineering Education." *Engineering Education,* 1988, *78*(7), 674–681.

Felder, R. "Reaching the Second Tier: Learning and Teaching Styles in College Science Education." *Journal of College Science Teaching,* 1993, *23*(5), 286–290.

Finkelstein, J. *Learning in Real Time: Synchronous Teaching and Learning Online.* San Francisco: Jossey-Bass, 2006.

Garrison, D., Anderson, T., and Archer, W. "Critical Thinking, Cognitive Presence and Computing Conferencing in Distance Education." *American Journal of Distance Education,* 2001, *15*(1), 7–23.

Kalyuga, S., Chandler, P., and Sweller, J. "Managing Split-Attention and Redundancy in Multimedia Instruction." *Applied Cognitive Psychology,* 1999, *13*(4), 351–371.

Kruse, K. "Designing eLearning User Interfaces Part 1: Assisting User Memory—Brain Memory." 2005. http://www.e-learningguru.com/articles/art4_2.htm.

Lewis, A. *The Seven Minute Difference: Small Steps to Big Changes.* New York: Kaplan, 2006.

Marsh, R., Sebrechts, M., Hicks, J., and Landau, J. "Processing Strategies and Secondary Memory in Very Rapid Forgetting." *Memory and Cognition,* 1997, *25,* 174–181.

Merrill, M. "First Principles of Instruction." *Educational Technology Research and Development,* 2002, *50*(3), 43–59.

Miller, G. "The Magical Number Seven, Plus or Minus Two: Some Limits on Our Capacity for Processing Information." *Psychological Review,* 1956, *63,* 81–97.

Moreno, R. "Animated Pedagogical Agents in Educational Technology." *Educational Technology,* 2004, *44*(6), 23–30.

Paivio, A. *Mental Representations: A Dual Coding Approach.* New York: Oxford University Press, 1986.

Palloff, R., and Pratt, K. *Collaborating Online: Learning Together in Community.* San Francisco: Jossey-Bass, 2005.

Palloff, R., and Pratt, K. *Building Online Communities: Effective Strategies for the Virtual Classroom.* San Francisco: Jossey-Bass, 2007.

Pomales-Garcia, C., and Liu, Y, "Web-Based Distance Learning Technology: The Impacts of Web Modules' Length and Format." *American Journal of Distance Education,* 2006, *20*(3), 163–179.

Steen, R. *The Evolving Brain: The Known and the Unknown.* Amherst, N.Y.: Prometheus Books, 2007.

Tobias, S. *They're Not Dumb, They're Different: Stalking the Second Tier.* Washington, D.C.: Science News Books, 1991.

Walvoord, B., and Anderson, V. *Effective Grading: A Tool for Learning and Assessment.* San Francisco: Jossey-Bass, 1998.

Weimer, M. *Learner-Centered Teaching: Five Key Changes to Practice.* San Francisco: Jossey-Bass, 2002.

Wu, H. K., and Shah, P. "Exploring Visuo-Spatial Thinking in Chemistry Learning." *Science Education,* 2004, *88,* 465–492.

Index

A

Action steps: designing for future course adaptation, 31–32; designing for learning, 17–19; designing in context of assessment, 43–45; documenting for tracking course issues, 101; organizing course development, 61; organizing student assignments, 91

Advanced planning, 17

American Association of Higher Education Assessment Forum, 34

Angel, 100

Around-the-clock access, 14

Assessment: authentic, 36–37; importance of, 34–35; providing self-assessment opportunities, 35–36, 52–53; using quizzes for, 35, 37; teaching in context of, 38–41. *See also* Evaluation

Assignments: communicating appropriate pace for completing, 88–89; consistent policies for turning in, 85; designed for each module, 25; establishing due dates for, 84, 85; establishing point system for, 52; instructions for discussion, 89–90, 98; maintaining list of revisions made in, 98–99; naming scheme for organizing, 91; tips for first time Web-based instructors on, 42

Association of American Medical Colleges, 19

Authentic assessment, 36–37

Awalt, C., 5

B

Behavioral self-assessment format, 53

Blackboard, 100

Blog, 97–98

Boettcher, J., 16

Building Online Communities: Effective Strategies for the Virtual Classroom (Palloff and Pratt), 101

C

Call log (Form 9), 95–96

Chickering, A., 6, 7, 34, 52

Chunk-ability, 14

Chunking, 64, 66–81

Classroom courses: differences between online and, 4–5; equal to online coursework, 11; similarities between online and, 4–5

N

Naming schemes: creating online course, 29–30; for student assignments, 91

Navigation: consistency between module, 85; documenting for revisions in, 96–99; giving student access to module components, 94–95; learning management system, 100; link rot and, 99–100, 101

O

Online course design: arranging for review of, 90–91; continuous improvement as part of, 95–96; facilitating future updating or adaptation, 21–32; keeping assessment in mind, 33–45; to maximize learning, 1–19; of navigation procedures, 85, 93–101; organizational aspects of, 47–61; with process in mind, 83–91

Online courses: advantages to having, 5–6; altered learning environment of, 12–13; creating file system and naming schemes for, 29–30; equal to classroom coursework, 11; faculty member's role in, 15; FAQs list on, 97; learner-centered environment of, 13–14; navigation through, 85, 93–101; organization of, 47–61; reviewing, 90–91; student's role in, 14–15. *See also* Modules; Revising online courses

Online learning: differences between classroom and, 4–5; similarities between classroom and, 6–7

Organization: action steps for, 61; of course equipment, 58; of folder and file system, 30–32; of instructional guidance, 60; learning guide, 25,

27–29, 48–53; naming scheme for assignment, 91; preparation time aspect of, 55; prioritizing your tasks for, 53–57; resource gathering, 57; selecting the most important topics, 59–60; use of technology, 58–59

P

Pace issue, 14

Palloff, R., 101

Pause-ability, 15

Place issue, 14

Planning: asking for information as part of, 22–23; benefits of advanced, 17; schedule of course due dates, 84

Pratt, K., 101

Preparation time, 55

Prioritization: course development tasks, 53–55; decision making for, 55–57

Priority triangle, 55–56*fig*

Q

Quizzes: designed for each module, 25; establishing point system for, 52; organizing the course, 57; providing self-assessment through, 35, 37, 53

R

Repeat-ability, 14

Reviewing course procedures, 90–91

Revising online courses: continuous improvement implemented when, 95–96; creating the outline for, 24–25; documentation used to facilitate, 96–99; file and folder systems to facilitate, 29–31; keeping list of issues/revisions of, 97; learning guide to facilitate, 25, 27–29; preparing in advance for, 23–24. *See also* Online courses

S

Scheduling: developing course due dates, 84; facilitating convenience element of course, 84–85; by individual students, 13; prioritizing in creating your course, 53–55; rewards of preparation time, 55; of teaching online courses, 28

Self-assessment: creating opportunities for, 52–53; different formats available for, 35–36, 53

Self-selected schedule, 13

Steen, R., 59

Student messages: consistent availability and response to, 85–86; prioritizing order of responses to, 86–88

Students: advanced planning by, 17; "coffee shop" forum for interactions between, 88; distractions confronted by online, 11–12; keeping scheduling convenient for, 84–85; learning environments which engage, 7; learning styles of, 8–11; maintaining file of suggestions made by, 97; providing instructional guidance tips for, 60; self-assessment by, 35–36; tracking "high-maintenance," 96; verifying work/testing by, 42–43. *See also* Faculty

T

Teaching: for the long term, 38–41; for transfer of knowledge, 16–17

Teaching style: in context of learning, 11; Felder's definition of, 10

Technological equipment, 58–59

Telephone communication, 88

Testing: designed for each module, 25; establishing point system for, 52; providing self-assessment through, 35; strategies for assessment using, 37; tips for first time Web-based instructors on, 42–43

Textbooks: avoid embedding page numbers in course content, 27; converting chapter numbers to Form 4 topics, 29

Time scheduling. *See* Scheduling

Tobias, S., 8

Topics: assigning quizzes/assignments for individual, 25; choosing the most important, 59–60; naming schemes for, 29–30. *See also* Content

Transfer of knowledge: course development and design for, 15–16; course facilitation and teaching for, 16–17. *See also* Learning

U

Understand-ability, 15

V

VARK Learning Styles Inventory, 8–9

W

Web-based courses. *See* Online courses

WebCT, 58, 91, 100

Web sites: Felder's Inventory, 8; Lolaexchange, 19; MedEdPORTAL, 19; Merlot, 18; MIT OpenCourseWare, 19; VARK Learning Styles Inventory, 8, 9; World Lecture Hall, 18

Weimer, M., 22, 58, 101

Wesleyan University, 19

World Lecture Hall, 18

The Jossey-Bass Guides to Online Teaching & Learning

Engaging the Online Learner
Activities and Resources for Creative Instruction

By Rita-Marie Conrad & J. Ana Donaldson

978-0-7879-6667-6 | Paper | 144 pp. | $27.00

The first title in the Jossey-Bass Guides to Online Teaching and Learning series, *Engaging the Online Learner* includes an innovative framework that helps learners become more involved as knowledge generators and co-facilitators of a course. The book also provides specific ideas for tested activities that can go a long way to improving online learning

Collaborating Online
Learning Together in Community

By Rena M. Palloff and Keith Pratt

978-0-7879-7614-9 | Paper | 128 pp. | $27.00

The second title in the Jossey-Bass Guides to Online Teaching and Learning series, *Collaborating Online* provides practical guidance for faculty seeking to help their students work together in creative ways, move out of the box of traditional papers and projects, and deepen the learning experience through their work with one another.

Exploring the Digital Library
A Guide for Online Teaching and Learning

By Kay Johnson & Elaine Magusin

978-0-7879-7627-9 | Paper | 176 pp. | $27.00

The third title in the Jossey-Bass Guides to Online Teaching and Learning series, *Exploring the Digital Library* addresses the key issue of library services for faculty and their students in the online learning environment. This book shows how faculty can effectively use digital libraries in their day-to-day work and in the design of electronic courses.

Learning in Real Time
Synchronous Teaching and Learning Online

By Jonathan E. Finkelstein

978-0-7879-7921-8 | Paper | 176 pp. | $27.00

The fourth book in the Jossey-Bass Guides to Online Teaching and Learning series, *Learning in Real Time* offers keen insight into the world of synchronous learning tools, guides instructors in evaluating how and when to use them, and illustrates how educators can develop their own strategies and styles in implementing such tools to improve online learning.